VERMONT COLLEGE
MONTPELIER, VT.

WITHDRAWN

THE MODERN NATIONS IN
HISTORICAL PERSPECTIVE

ROBIN W. WINKS, *General Editor*

The volumes in this series deal with individual nations or groups of closely related nations throughout the world, summarizing the chief historical trends and influences that have contributed to each nation's present-day character, problems, and behavior. Recent data are incorporated with established historical background to achieve a fresh synthesis and original interpretation.

The author of this volume, ROBERT V. DANIELS, has written a number of books on Russia and Communism, including A *Documentary History of Communism, The Conscience of the Revolution: Communist Opposition in Soviet Russia,* and *The Nature of Communism.* He is fluent in Russian and has travelled in the Soviet Union. A graduate of Harvard University, where he received his M.A. and Ph.D. degrees, Dr. Daniels is at present Professor of History at the University of Vermont.

FORTHCOMING EUROPEAN VOLUMES

Austria and Hungary *by R. John Rath*
The Balkans *by Charles and Barbara Jelavich*
East Central Europe *by Frederick G. Heymann*
France *by John C. Cairns*
Great Britain *by Norman Cantor*
Ireland *by Oliver MacDonagh*
Italy *by Massimo Salvadori*
Scandinavia *by John H. Wuorinen*
Spain *by Richard Herr*

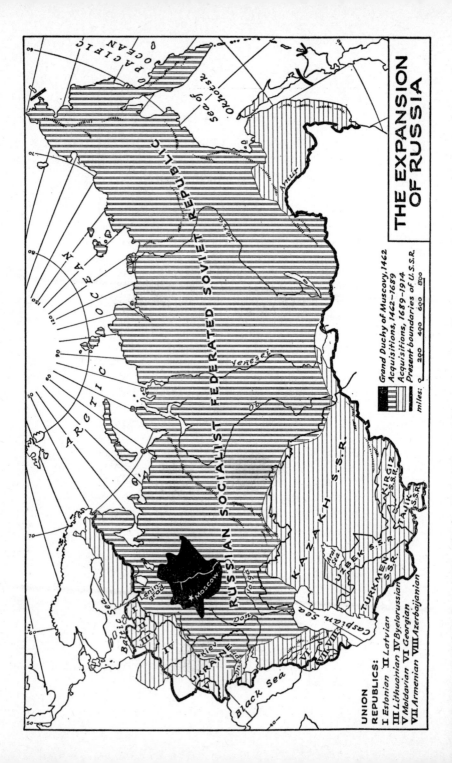

THE EXPANSION
OF RUSSIA

Grand Duchy of Muscovy, 1462
Acquisitions, 1462-1689
Acquisitions, 1689-1914
Present boundaries of U.S.S.R.

miles: 0   200   400   600   800

UNION
REPUBLICS:
I Estonian   II Latvian
III Lithuanian IV Byelorussian
V Moldavian   VI Georgian
VII Armenian VIII Azerbaijanian

RUSSIA

Robert V. Daniels

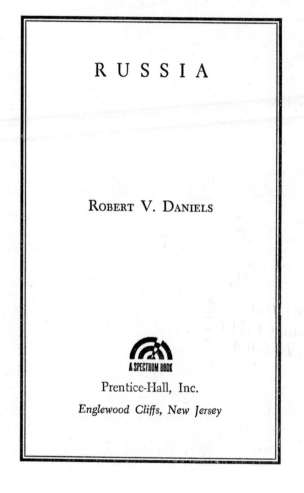

A SPECTRUM BOOK

Prentice-Hall, Inc.

Englewood Cliffs, New Jersey

Copyright © 1964 by PRENTICE-HALL, INC., *Englewood Cliffs, N.J.*

All rights reserved. No part of this book may be reproduced in any form, by mimeograph or any other means, without permission in writing from the publishers.

Library of Congress Catalog Card Number 64-23568.
Printed in the United States of America—C.

P 78449,
C 78450

947
D186r

PREFACE

The modern world has grown so bewilderingly complex that it is virtually impossible for the ordinary reader to understand the forces that shape international events. What is all too often lacking, amidst the plethora of news reports and conflicting interpretations, is a clear and comprehensive presentation of the historical background of current world problems.

Soviet Russia, because of its critical role in world affairs, and because its character, to the Westerner, seems so contradictory and confusing, is especially in need of clear historical explanation. This book presents an historical summary and analysis of what Soviet Russia is, how it got that way, and how it appears to be changing. Of course, one small volume cannot possibly include all that is worth knowing about so complex and important a nation. The reader who is interested in further study is referred to the annotated list of Suggested Readings at the end of this book.

It is my hope that this short survey of Russia will be a suitable introduction for the general reader, whether he is enrolled in a formal course of study or is pursuing the subject on his own. It should prove useful to students in introductory college history courses and in advanced high school courses who wish to begin a study of Russia. It may also be helpful for students of political science, economics, sociology, and geography who want further reading on the Russian side of their subject. Lastly, it may be of use to people already interested in some aspect of present-day Russia —politics, economics, culture, or the language—who want to review the historical background of Russian society.

Russian history is complicated by the frequency of place-name changes and by the system of "Old Style" dates, thirteen days behind the Gregorian calendar of the West, that prevailed until February 1918. My practice is to employ the names and dates in use at the particular time referred to: thus, "St. Petersburg" to 1914, "Petrograd" to 1924, "Leningrad" since; "February Revolution" and "October Revolution" (began October 25, 1917, O.S., or November 7, N.S.).

16671

I am indebted to Professor Firuz Kazemzadeh of Yale University for his very helpful critique of the manuscript. I wish to acknowledge my obligation to the University of Vermont and the Rockefeller Foundation for their support of my research work during the period when this book was in preparation. Finally, my thanks go to Mrs. Katherine Marston for research assistance on many details and to Miss Carole Sanders for typing the manuscript.

R.V.D.

(Postscript)
October 16, 1964

This book was going to press when the world was stunned by the news of the fall of Nikita Khrushchev from his positions as head of the Soviet government and the Communist Party of the Soviet Union. If, as it appears, he was removed by a vote of the party Presidium or the central committee, this was the first time in the history of Russia that the established ruler was voted out of office. Khrushchev's successors—Leonid Brezhnev as First Secretary of the Party and Aleksei Kosygin as Premier in the government—cannot immediately, if ever, succeed to the measure of personal power that Khrushchev apparently had at his height. Otherwise, there is as yet no indication of any radical change in the domestic structure or foreign policy of the Soviet regime.

Contents

ONE The Soviet Union Today   1
*The Soviet Union in Its International Setting, 1;
The Soviet Political System, 8; The Soviet Econ-
omy and Soviet Society, 17; Soviet Thought and
Culture, 21; The Nature of the Soviet System, 26*

TWO The Russian Past   27
*The Rise of the Russian Nation, 27; The Russian
Autocracy, 33; Backwardness and Bondage in Rus-
sian Society, 40; Russian Culture: Orthodoxy vs.
Westernization, 45; The Russian Past and the
Soviet State, 53*

THREE The Revolution   56
*The Nature of Revolution, 56; The Background of
Revolution in Russia, 60; Marxism, 63; Toward
the Collapse of Tsarism, 68; 1917, 72; The Revolution and the Soviet System, 82*

FOUR The Evolution of the Soviet System   96
*The New Economic Policy and the Succession
Struggle, 97; The Stalin Revolution and Its After-
math, 104; The Transformation of Soviet Thought
and Society, 111; Stalinism Triumphant, 115; The
Succession and the Khrushchev Era, 119*

FIVE Soviet Russia and the World   125
*Soviet Russia in Isolation, 125; Soviet Russia in
Alliance, 128; Soviet Russia and the Blocs, 133*

Suggested Readings   141

Index   147

RUSSIA'S WESTERN BORDER

Boundary of 1725
Boundary of 1914
Boundary, 1921-1939
1964 National boundary
Boundaries of Union Republics

ONE

THE SOVIET UNION TODAY

The Union of Soviet Socialist Republics is more than a country. It is not one nation, but an empire embracing many large and small national minorities. The Russians make up scarcely 50 per cent of the population. Further, the USSR is the center of the world-wide political movement of the Communist parties. Its position in the Communist movement affords it substantial influence over the destinies of the other countries under Communist rule. Finally, the USSR is, together with the United States of America, one of the world's two superpowers whose superiority in economic and military strength in this nuclear age places in their hands the fate of the entire globe.

As a starting point for the historical interpretation of Soviet Russia, this initial chapter is devoted to a summary of the Soviet system and its international setting today. We will begin with an appraisal of the USSR's international power and policies, proceed to an analysis of the Soviet political structure, and then go on to an evaluation of the nature and development of the Soviet economy, society, and culture. Throughout, we will be concerned with the relation of the Soviet Union to the world-wide ideological movement of Communism, and with the factors of Russian history which appear to have influenced present Soviet realities. In subsequent chapters we will consider the whole span of prerevolutionary history, the cataclysm of the revolutionary years, the historical development of the Soviet regime itself, and the evolving relationships of the Soviet Union with the outside world. Our hope is to arrive at a balanced presentation of the historical roots of the Soviet system and of the forces that are moving it.

The Soviet Union in Its International Setting

The international power of the Soviet Union and the problems this poses for the rest of the world are the end product of several centuries of the most remarkably steady political rise. From a scattering of principalities under foreign yoke or barbarian terror, Russia rose to become a national state, a multinational empire, and a major power among the great states of Europe. Finally, from the long world conflict of 1914-1945 Russia emerged as one of the two super-powers that froze world politics into the anxious balance of two nuclear-armed camps.

Any nation's power in international affairs depends on how it rates in terms of a few basic sources of strength. These we might classify under the headings of (1) population; (2) territorial resources and strategic location; (3) level of economic and technological development; (4) effectiveness of governmental authority; and (5) the will to mobilize these assets in order to maximize the nation's international influence.

Soviet Russia's population of 209 million people (according to the census of 1959) is surpassed only by the 400 million of India and the 700 million of China. Russia has had the largest population in Europe ever since the country's rapid (and still not fully explained) population increase commenced in the middle of the eighteenth century.

The Soviet Union, strategically located in the heart of the vast Eurasian continent, has by far the largest area of any country in the world, comprising over one sixth of the earth's total land surface. It should be pointed out, however, that a very large part of Russia's territory is uninhabitable Arctic and sub-Arctic waste. Northern European Russia and the whole of Siberia, save its populated western wedge and its southern fringe along the Trans-Siberian Railroad, have little importance in the reckoning of national resources. In addition, most of Soviet Central Asia is a desert, as sparse in its resources and population as the American Southwest. The Soviet Union has about as much arable land as the United States or China, with a density of rural population much higher than in America though nowhere near as high as in China.*

Russia's past and present have been heavily influenced by geographical circumstance. The Russian climate—northern cold, continental extremes of summer and winter, mid-continental aridity—greatly restricts agricultural possibilities. The extremes of cold and dryness, progressively more severe to the eastward, have channeled the heaviest concentration of population into a long wedge, broad in European Russia but steadily narrowed by the limitations of cold

* An approximate index of rural population density per acre of arable land is as follows:
US—0.1; USSR—0.2; Great Britain—0.5; China—1.9; Japan—4.0.

winters and dry summers as one crosses the Urals and moves eastward through Siberia. This area of settlement corresponds roughly to the original vegetation zones of broadleaf or mixed forest and the prairie grasslands known as steppes. North of this is the evergreen forest, or taiga, still a barrier to cultivation. To the south is the dry steppe, which east of the Caspian Sea becomes outright desert.

The Russian steppes are flat and open and were easily accessible to nomadic horsemen. From time immemorial the steppes have witnessed wave after wave of invasions by an almost inexhaustible series of tribes moving out of Central Asia. Throughout most of its early history Russia had no natural frontiers; it was a vulnerable flat-land state which could command neither the mountain or maritime borders of the great Eurasian plain. By the eighteenth century Russia had expanded to certain natural limits: the Baltic and Black seas, the mountains of Transcaucasia, the Altai Mountains and their eastward extension, and the Pacific Ocean. Toward the west, however, the frontier remained less definite and fluctuated with the vicissitudes of war. Only since 1945 has it rested on a clear national division between the Poles to the west and the Soviet Ukrainians and Byelorussians to the east.

Certain strategic disadvantages in Russia's geographical position remain. Russia is an almost landlocked power. Its coastal regions— the Black Sea, the Caspian, the Baltic, the White Sea and Arctic Ocean, the Bering Sea, the Sea of Okhotsk, and the Sea of Japan— are widely separated and for the most part cut off from easy access to the open ocean. A traditional force in Russia's history has been the push toward the sea—the Black Sea and the Straits, the Baltic, and ice-free ports on the Pacific—but its achievement is far from complete.

Another major component of national power is the relative level of the economic and technological training and equipment of the people in comparison with their neighbors. In the case of Russia this factor is in turn dependent on the two political components of national power: the effectiveness of central governmental organization and the will to mobilize its sources of power.

One of the most striking features of Russian history is the disproportionate domination by the state over other aspects of life. Compared with Western Europe, the Russian state has wielded far more control over nongovernmental groups and institutions such as the Church, social classes, private property and business, and intellectual life. This was particularly the case after the termination of Mongol-Tatar overlordship in the fifteenth century, a time which also saw the formation of a strong national state in European Russia. The Russian national state was among the earliest in Europe, and more completely centralized. The absolutist tradition persisted throughout the period of imperial expansion from the sixteenth through the eighteenth centuries and gave the Russian government opportunity to develop the machinery for exacting from the population—servile peasant and conscript noble alike—the maximum military effort permitted by the low cultural and economic level of the country. In the nineteenth century the state lost some of its pre-eminence, but regained it more firmly than ever under the new Communist government after the Revolution. Soviet Russia continues to be, of all societies in the world, the one most fully mobilized in the service of the state.

In their will to use power Russia's rulers were always unsurpassed, though their motives were shared by most sovereigns who governed in the tradition of absolute monarchy. The nation was the possession of the monarch, his tool in the political game against rival kings and emperors. There was no limit to his ambitions, save the danger of a superior alliance against him and the need to have his own allies in order to forestall this. It was only this "balance of power" that gave international politics such stability as it had in the age of kings. The Soviet government has shown itself to be a vigorous heir of the tsarist tradition in its will to use power and its efforts to expand its territory and influence.

Backwardness in economy, technology, culture, thought, and education has marked Russia's history just as deeply as the country's relative precocity in the development of centralized governmental power. A major concern of the political authorities in Russia ever since the ninth century A.D. has been to stimulate—even if by force—the economic and cultural progress of the country in order to catch up with the superior civilizations to the south and west. Two hundred years of stagnation under the Mongols and Tatars put Russia still further behind the West. In the centuries that followed whatever progress the Russians made in alleviating ignorance and poverty was more than offset by the cultural gains of the burgeoning civilization of Western Europe. At the time of the Revolution Russia was still 50 to 100 years behind the West in the process of industrialization.

Much of the distinctive character of Soviet history and of the Communist institutions of Soviet Russia merely represents the modern version of the old Russian effort to solve the old Russian problem of economic and cultural lag by the old Russian methods of autocratic government. The results have been spectacular. Soviet Russia has built a vast, modern industrial plant and educated a hitherto backward peasant society in all the manifold technological skills of an industrial society. Though the interests of the individual citizen are still slighted and there are virtually no nongovernmental institutions, the Soviet state now has at its unrestricted command the modern resources of the world's second-largest industrial establishment.

While Soviet Russia has been growing in its capacity to exercise power in international affairs, the political environment of world power distribution has radically changed. Until World War II the key roles in international politics were played by a number of great powers: Germany, France, Britain, Italy, and Japan as well as the Soviet Union and the United States. World War II changed all this. Military defeat in World War II removed first France and then the Axis powers from the front ranks of world leadership. The USSR, through economic development, and the United States, by exercising its new-found will to act in world politics, moved into the political vacuum. The resultant bipolarity forced all the other powers to take their stand behind one of the two giants.

A new source of world tension is the revolutionary movement of international Communism which Soviet Russia has controlled and promoted. At first, international Communism actually had a negative effect on the expansion of Russian power and influence because it accentuated the hostility of the other great powers toward Russia. To be sure, the Russian Communists originally thought of themselves as the spark that would touch off the world revolutionary conflagration, and of Russia only as the temporary leader in this effort. Over the years, however, a profound transformation occurred in the Communist movement, such that the means—Russian national power—became the end, and the end—world-wide Communist revolution—became a tool in the service of Russian power.

Nevertheless, the Communist revolutionary movement (with some recent qualifications) is still an important instrument of Soviet power. The manner of its use has varied over time and in relation to the distance of the target from the Soviet Union. It took eight or ten years to mold the Communist International into a reliable servant of Soviet power. From the late 1920s until 1956 there was no challenge to Soviet control within the movement. Since then the movement has begun to come apart at its national seams, particularly with the growing discord between the Soviet Union and Communist China.

Until World War II Communist rule was confined to Soviet Russia and Outer Mongolia, and its influence otherwise had to be exerted through the revolutionary opposition parties which Communists created in almost every country of the world. Most of these parties have had only nuisance value, but in China, Germany, France, and Spain the Communists won enough influence at times either to push their governments into temporary alliance with Soviet Russia or to provoke the formation of violently anti-Russian, extreme right-wing governments.

Communist parties emerged from World War II with greatly enhanced strength in Europe and Asia and wherever possible were pressed into power as agents of Soviet influence. They were successful, however, only in areas under Soviet military occupation. In Poland, Czechoslovakia, Hungary, Rumania, Bulgaria, and finally East Germany, the Russians were able to set up satellite governments whose independence, until 1956, was only nominal. The same thing had been done in Outer Mongolia in the 1920s and was repeated in North Korea after 1945.

In certain countries not subject to direct Soviet military power Communist governments came to power on their own, thanks to the fortunes of World War II and its aftermath. In Yugoslavia, Albania, China, and Indochina the Russians reaped nothing but trouble, however, for these governments interpreted their Communist interests contrary to the wishes of the Soviet state and defied the Russians when it came to a showdown. Tito's Yugoslavia was able to escape from the Russian orbit and stand apart from both the Soviet and Western blocs. China, with its tremendous population, soon challenged the Russians with a new bipolarity within the Communist movement itself. Such is the shattering effect of a power conflict within an ideological movement that the Sino-Soviet dispute is splitting the world-wide movement into two separate kinds of Communism, each attached to its preferred great power, and bitterly hostile to one another.

Despite the Chinese problem and the pro-Chinese defections in the international Communist movement, the Soviet Union still enjoys the support of a legion of sympathizers abroad and the protection afforded by a fairly reliable band of satellite states in East Central Europe. But above all, Soviet power today rests on the armed might of the USSR itself and the industrial potential that stands behind it. The Soviet army, at 2,500,000, is the largest in the world, despite some recent reductions. The Soviet air force has some 20,000 operational combat planes, equal in quantity if not in quality to the air force of the United States. The Soviet navy, owing to the geographical peculiarities of the country, has a primarily defensive role and relies mainly on submarines, of which some 450 are presently thought to be operational.

Beyond all these conventional military forces stands the fearsome power of the hydrogen bomb and the intercontinental rocket which can hurl it toward any target in the world. Of this ultimate weapon the two superpowers presently have a near monopoly, qualified only by the token force of the British and the future projects of the French and the Chinese. The quantitative power of the American and Soviet nuclear stockpiles staggers the imagination; each country has enough explosive power to devastate the other many—who knows how many? —times over. It is these nuclear arsenals, indeed, that make the two superpowers loom so large above all their neighbors. Nuclear weapons represent, in turn, the military fruition of the world's two greatest industrial and scientific establishments.

Soviet behavior in the international community has shown a perplexing mixture of the traditional and the revolutionary. As the self-styled citadel of Marxism-Leninism, Soviet Russia has been since 1917 the active center of a militant international revolutionary creed, devoted to the vision of a world proletarian revolution and the creation of a Marxist utopia everywhere. But beneath the doctrinal façade it is possible to see how completely the movement has been identified with Russian national aspirations. It may eventually appear that the greatest effect Russia ever had on the world was to convert natural revolutionary movements everywhere into Russian-style autocracies of discipline and dogma.

In everyday diplomacy Russia's approach has oscillated between a devious search for allies and single-minded defiance of the whole anti-Communist world. Up to World War II the trend was toward conventional diplomacy. At the end of World War II the Soviet Union took every opportunity afforded by confusion and political chaos to thrust for maximum immediate gains with all the unscrupulousness of tsarism and Leninism combined. Since Stalin's death in 1953 a new attitude of moderation has prevailed, as the Soviet Union has tried to balance its waning hold on the Communist bloc countries with an appeal to the neutral ex-colonial states.

Soviet Russia, like America, faces the prospect of an increasingly fluid international situation. The two major blocs are crumbling. Neutrals are growing in number and influence and have to be courted with cultural delegations, educational exchanges, and economic aid. The Soviet Union is under particular pressure to make a good impression on uncommitted nations, and this requires more domestic reform and an un-Leninist sophistication internationally. Finally, there are forces in motion that may soon challenge the pre-eminence of the two superpowers, as other governments—China and the Franco-German combination—approach the time when they too can threaten the world with nuclear weapons.

The Soviet Political System

Soviet Russia is a totalitarian state. The Soviet political system shares with various other regimes of the present and recent past the basic features which distinguish the uniquely modern phenomenon of totalitarianism. Totalitarianism, to put it simply, is a system in which all power is in the hands of the state and the state is in the hands of a dictator. It differs from the absolute monarchies of old in several ways. It is revolutionary rather than traditional and must rely on coercion and terror more than on custom to secure obedience. Totalitarianism means not only a monopoly of political power in the hands of the ruler, but intimate control by the political authority over all nongovernmental groups, institutions, and activities, be they economic, social, religious, or intellectual. Totalitarianism means a system in which there are no restraints of law or custom on the actions of those in authority or on their power to crush all sources of opposition.

The key feature of a totalitarian regime is the institution known as the party. The totalitarian party is an invention of the Russian Bolsheviks, fashioned on the disciplinary and dogmatic Leninist lines of a military priesthood whose purpose is to seize governmental power. After the Russian Revolution the party became a permanent and supreme agency of rule. The Russian model was copied by all the other totalitarian movements:—Communist, fascist, and non-Western nationalist.

The totalitarian party is a highly centralized, authoritarian organization whose membership is bound to carry out the orders of the leadership and the full-time party officials, even though in some cases the forms of democratic procedure may be retained as window dressing. Party members in turn control every other institution in society, including the regular machinery of government, since all opposition to the party is suppressed by the political police. Through the party machine, its subsidiary organizations ("transmission belts"), and all the other organizations which the party controls, the leader or leaders of the party can impose their will absolutely and arbitrarily. The totalitarian party takes particular pains to control all channels of public thought and communication by monopolizing the modern mass media of the press and broadcasting and education and by imposing the party's ideology or official code of belief on everything spoken or printed in public. Totalitarian leaders accentuate international hostility through their messianic aggressiveness or fanatic nationalism, and in turn capitalize on international tension as an excuse for maintaining their power.

The basic political similarity among the various totalitarian systems should not obscure the substantial differences of doctrine and policy among the totalitarianisms of the Left, Right, and Center, and even among the different national varieties of Communism: Soviet, Chinese, Yugoslav, Polish, and so on. Communism is poles apart from fascism in its ideology and in the emotions to which it appeals prior to its acquisition of power. Fascism was more nakedly nationalist, aggressive, and sadistic. Communism professes to be the true heir to the Western tradition of democratic humanism, while fascism frankly repudiated all the values of that tradition. In this respect Communism suffers from a greater discrepancy between theory and practice; it is hypocritical, and it has greater problems of enforcing mass belief in its official doctrine.

In social and economic life as well Communist totalitarianism involves much more complete and systematic party and governmental control than do the other forms of totalitarianism. The Communist economy is completely, or almost completely, state-owned—i.e., socialistic—whereas the fascist economy was basically capitalistic, with government regulation superimposed.

The sources from which Communist totalitarianism arose in Russia are manifold, and an analysis of them leads far back into the history of Russia. To a substantial degree Russian society was already prone to totalitarian controls because of the preponderance of autocratic state power in Russia's historical development. On top of this, any great revolution leads almost inevitably to dictatorship. Revolutionary dictatorship in the twentieth century, with all the resources of modern organization, weapons, and mass media at its disposal, can hardly avoid becoming totalitarian. Finally, we must take into account the personal power drive of Vladimir Lenin and the military nature of the Bolshevik Party which he developed. It was the party as an institution which nurtured the potential for totalitarianism inherent in the Russian revolutionary situation and brought it to its pinnacle in the terror-ridden reign of Joseph Stalin.

The Communist Party of the Soviet Union, like its counterparts in the other Communist countries, is nominally a nongovernmental organization, but it enjoys the *de facto* monopoly of political activity and in practice exercises many of the functions of government. The 10 million or more members of the CPSU are the privileged elite in Soviet society. While the Party includes a fair number of workers and peasants or collective farm officials, managerial personnel comprise a greater proportion of the membership, and at the top echelon in every organization or activity practically everyone must be a member of the Party.

The Party membership is not, however, a true ruling class. It has no real privilege of decision making and must submit to the strict discipline imposed by the Party "apparatus." The apparatus is the central and local organization of full-time Party officials—Party secretaries and their employees—which transmits authority from the top down through the membership and actually carries out the function of totalitarian control over the rest of society.

Theoretically, the internal organization of the Party is perfectly democratic (see Figure 1). The basic unit is the Primary Party Organization, consisting of the members in a given factory, office, military unit, etc. The P.P.O. elects a secretary, who, if his unit is a big one, will work full time on a salary. From the P.P.O. delegates are chosen to a district or city Party conference, which elects the Party Committee and a full-time secretary for that locality. Local delegates go to Party conferences in each province or each national minority region and similarly elect committees, bureaus, and secretaries for the larger territorial unit. Finally, provincial delegates, to the number of some 2,000, assemble for the All-Union Party Congress (now supposed to be held once every three years), and there they elect the Central Committee, the Party Presidium, and the Secretariat. The Party Congress is supposed to be the highest policy-making body of the Party. In the interim, supreme authority theoretically rests with the Central Committee (175 members and 155 alternates), while day-to-day policy decisions are made by the Presidium (12 members and 6 alternates). Organizational questions are handled by the Secretariat (13 members). The top office in the Party is the post of First Secretary, currently held by Nikita Khrushchev.

The power structure of the Party is entirely contrary to its form on paper. Ever since Stalin's rise to power in the 1920s the First Secretary (then called General Secretary) has had the *de facto* power of appointing the full-time Party secretaries all down the line. The secretaries in turn control the very Party members and committees to whom they are nominally responsible. The secretaries enforce rules of strict adherence to Party discipline and to the decisions of the top authorities. Any member who objects is subject to expulsion from

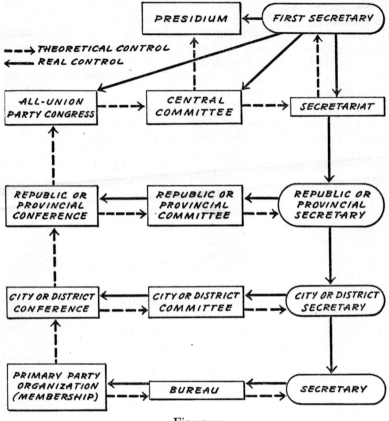

Figure 1

ORGANIZATION OF THE CPSU

the Party, and since the Party has a political monopoly, expulsion means political oblivion, if not a worse fate at the hands of the secret police. By means of this bureaucratic system of control through the hierarchy of secretaries, the First Secretary can pack all the Party committees and conferences with the men he wants, and hence he can easily control even the all-Union Congress and the Central Committee, which nominally elects the First Secretary himself. This system of circular control within the Party is the secret of the personal dictatorship exercised by Stalin from the late 1920s to 1953 and by Khrushchev from 1957 to 1964.

The Communist Party leaders exert the Party's influence on the government and society in two ways: by control down through the Party apparatus, and by the direct authority of the top Party members who head the government and all other important institutions. The top governmental officials are simultaneously members of the Party Presidium. Khrushchev headed the government as well as the Party by virtue of his position as Chairman of the Council of Ministers (i.e., Prime Minister). Thus, he combined in his own person the two highest seats of political power in the Soviet system. Other officials in the Party Presidium were Anastas Mikoyan, Chairman of the Presidium of the Supreme Soviet and thus nominal Head of State; Alexei Kosygin, First Deputy Prime Minister; Dmitri Polyansky, Deputy Prime Minister; Gennady Voronov, Prime Minister of the Russian Republic; Nikolai Shvernik, former Head of State; Andrei Kirilenko, Supervisor of Party Organization in the Russian Republic; and the four top-ranking colleagues of Khrushchev in the Party Secretariat: Leonid Brezhnev, Frol Kozlov (who has been ill since 1963), Mikhail Suslov, and Nikolai Podgorny. Most of the government ministers, military chiefs, and heads of institutions such as the trade unions and the Academy of Sciences are members of the Central Committee. All other key officials down the line are members of the local Party committees. The central Secretariat maintains a large staff to supervise the operations of government, industry, and agriculture, and particularly to control the indoctrination and propaganda which is a major responsibility of the local Party organizations and the mass media. Discipline and efficiency throughout the Soviet system are now overseen by the new Commission of Party and State Control, headed by the former police supervisor, Alexander Shelepin.

The weak spot in the system of Communist Party rule is the problem of succession when the dictator dies. Since the dictator's supreme authority is not legally recognized, there is no way to provide legally for its transfer to a new man. In the succession crises that followed the deaths of Lenin in 1924 and of Stalin in 1953, a "collective leadership" of the Presidium (formerly called the Politburo) took over until the key man in the Party organization (Stalin in the earlier instance, Khrushchev more recently) worked his way up by means of behind-the-scenes bureaucratic politics and finally got rid of all his rivals. Prospects are good that the succession after Khrushchev will be settled in the same way.

The government of the Soviet Union, like the Communist Party, is democratic in form and dictatorial in reality (see Figure 2). Soviet Russia has a written constitution (the present version dating from

(Khrushchev) are nominally responsible to the Supreme Soviet, as in the West European parliamentary system.

Since the Communist Party is an exclusive authoritarian organization furnishing or controlling the decisions of government at all levels, the democratic appearances of the Soviet government are a complete sham. Elections are meaningless because the Communist Party controls all nominations (of Party members or reliable nonmembers), and the voter has only the single candidate to accept or reject. Legislative assemblies at all levels—including the Supreme Soviet—have nothing to do but rubber-stamp the decisions of the executive organs, who in turn are simply applying the directives of the top Communist leadership.

A unique feature of the Soviet government is its federal organization, which reflects the multinational character of the Soviet Union. Great Russians—those who speak the Russian language—comprise only a little over half the Soviet population of some 220,000,000. Russian imperial expansion since the sixteenth century has brought within the present boundaries of the USSR millions of people of other nationalities, representing over a hundred different languages and dialects. These people were forcibly incorporated into the Russian Empire and were subjected to various forms of discrimination and oppression. When the Communists fell heir to the Russian multinational state they promised to respect the rights of national minorities, and though they barred any movement toward genuine independence, they did incorporate national identities and languages into the administrative structure of the country (see Figure 3). This was worked out in 1922 with the establishment of the Union of Socialist Republics, made up of union republics for each of the major nationality groups in the country. Smaller nationalities are recognized in the special provincial or local governments known as autonomous republics, autonomous regions, and national areas (the last a sort of glorified Indian Reservation for the Siberian aborigines).

At the present time the USSR comprises 15 union republics. By far the largest both in area and in population is the Russian Socialist Federated Soviet Republic, with a population in 1959 of 117.5 million, five-sixths Russian speaking and the remainder representing many small nationalities pocketed within Great Russia. Two other republics speak Slavic languages closely akin to Russian: the Ukraine (41.9 million), and Byelorussia or White Russia—not to be confused with the political White Russians who fought the Communists— (8.1 million). In Transcaucasia there are three republics: Georgia (4 million), Armenia (1.8 million), and Turkic-speaking Azerbaijan (3.7

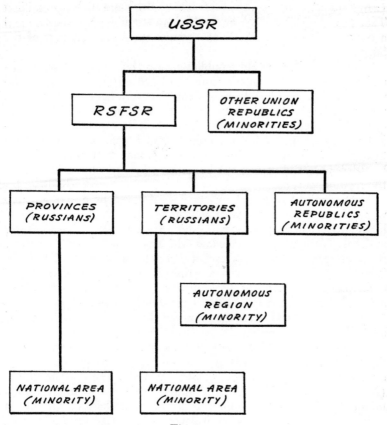

Figure 3

NATIONALITY STRUCTURE OF THE USSR

million). Four more republics, whose inhabitants speak Turkic languages, are located in Central Asia: Kazakhstan, occupying a large area of steppe and desert (9.3 million, more than half of whom are Russians and Ukrainians); Kirgizia (2.1 million); Uzbekistan (8.1 million); and Turkmenia (1.5 million). The fifth Central Asian republic, on the Afghan border, is Iranian-speaking Tajikistan (2 million). Finally, there are the four western republics annexed during World War II: the three Baltic states of Estonia (1.2 million), Latvia (2.1 million), and Lithuania (2.7 million), and the Rumanian-speaking province of Bessarabia, which is called the Moldavian Republic

(2.9 million). Other important nationalities are the five million Tatars on the Volga River in the Russian Republic and the two and a quarter million Jews scattered through the European part of the Soviet Union.

Theoretically, the union republics govern their own internal affairs and have the right to secede from the USSR. However, the governments of the republics, like the federal government of the USSR, are controlled by the Communist Party, and the units of the Party in the republics are strictly subordinate branches of the CPSU, subject to control from Moscow. Policies and propaganda are uniform throughout the entire union, though they may be expressed in the local language and carried out by native officials in the ministries of the republic governments.

The individual in Soviet society is confronted by a complex network of controls and pressures which increase in severity the more highly placed he is in the social system. He is subject to the ordinary authority of the police and the law, which now operate with relatively fair and regular procedures except for political offenses. Unless he is a collective farmer the average citizen is an employee of some governmental organization or government-owned institution. If he is in a responsible position he is subject constantly to the scrutiny of the Communist Party. He lives always under the shadow of that essential adjunct of totalitarianism, the political police.

The police are divided into two branches. The secret police, intelligence agents, border guards, and paramilitary internal security troops operate under the Committee of State Security. The ordinary police (Militia) are administered by the Ministry of Internal Affairs in each union republic. Under Stalin the police forces became virtually a state within the state, as an instrument of mass terror, but the Khrushchev regime prides itself on keeping the police under close Party control and avoiding groundless arrests.

Soviet justice operates with a hierarchy of higher and lower courts headed by the Supreme Court of the USSR and governed by an extensive body of law codes and decrees. Criminal cases are decided by the People's Courts, consisting of one professional judge and two "elected" assistants in lieu of a jury. Political crimes, involving alleged anti-Soviet or counterrevolutionary activity, are judged by military tribunals. There is also extensive litigation of civil cases, especially involving rights and contracts between different governmental agencies and enterprises. A unique Soviet institution is the office of the Procurator General, who is supposed to check on the legality of all the acts of the courts and the agencies of government—adhering, of course, to the basic policies of the Communist Party leaders.

Although the present conduct of the Soviet government and the Communist Party is less violent or capricious than it has been at times in the past, the fundamental controls of the totalitarian state remain. Despite the extensive economic, social, and educational development of the Soviet Union under the direction of the Communist Party, there is little prospect of any real reduction in the totalitarian powers of the regime or of any substantial change in the centralized control of economic and intellectual life. Tensions exist, to be sure, between the Party apparatus and managers and specialists in other fields of activity, and they will probably increase. Nevertheless, there is little reason to doubt that the Communist Party organization, barring some international catastrophe, can perpetuate its power within the Soviet Union indefinitely.

The Soviet Economy and Soviet Society

The Soviet economic system is based on the principle of state socialism—that is, complete governmental ownership or control and highly centralized planning of all economic activity. All factories, transport and communication facilities, mines, most stores, and many farms are owned outright by the government, whether they were nationalized at the time of the Revolution or constructed subsequently. A few stores and service establishments and all the collective farms are technically cooperatives belonging to their members, but these too are under strict Party and governmental control. Any private enterprise involving the hiring of labor or the reselling of goods is illegal, on the grounds that it is exploitation or speculation. About the only self-employed people are writers, some professional men who work on contract, and a few individual artisans.

Control over the state-owned industry of the USSR is divided between the central authorities and the economic councils in each of some 40 economic regions and minority republics. Prior to the reform of 1957 each branch of large-scale industry was administered by a special ministry in Moscow, with over-all coordination and planning vested in the State Planning Commission. Transport, communications, and the armament industry, as well as planning work, are still centralized in Moscow, but jurisdiction over most branches of industrial production is now vested in the regional councils.

The organization and operation of the individual Soviet factory or other enterprise differs little from the practice of a large-scale establishment in any industrialized society. Contrary to the Marxist ideal of the equalitarian collective, the Soviet enterprise is based on the familiar hierarchy of skill, responsibility, and reward, from workmen through foremen to executives. Workers are usually paid on a piece-work incentive basis, with average real wages from a half to a quarter of the West European and American levels. A manager draws much higher pay, together with substantial bonuses if his enterprise fulfills its production plan.

Trade unions exist—under firm Communist Party control—but they have no right to strike or to negotiate on wages, which are determined by the government. The chief function of the trade unions is to exert Party influence on the non-Party workers and to campaign for greater productivity. Secondarily, they are entrusted with the administration of social benefits: housing (which is still in short supply), vacations, and the social security system of sickness and retirement payments.

The entire Soviet economy is governed by the plan. Comprehensive, long-term planning of current production and new construction has been in force ever since Stalin initiated the First Five-Year Plan in 1929. In 1959 a Seven-Year Plan went into effect. Under it each enterprise is assigned monthly and yearly production quotas, while money and materials are allocated to assure fulfillment of the plan. Enterprise managers and higher industrial officials are under great pressure from the Communist Party organization, which has over-all responsibility to see that the plan is fulfilled in each district and region. Local officials are blamed for failure to fulfill even if the deficiency is due to errors in the allocation of materials by higher authorities. There is a chronic problem with local officials who falsify records and pretend to have fulfilled the plan or who embezzle enterprise funds and materials for their own profit. The entire Soviet administrative system suffers from overcentralization of authority and a lack of local initiative on the part of officials who are fearful of violating central policy or regulations. The plan really functions as a system of targets or goals, set up to evoke the maximum effort from everyone in the whole society.

In certain fields the results of the Soviet system of planned production and industrial construction are very impressive. Those areas of the economy that have received preference in the allocation of money and materials—above all, the area of heavy industry such as mining, steel, machinery manufacturing, and the armament industry —have developed at an extraordinary rate. Soviet steel production, to take the key indicator, was scarcely above the pre-World War I level of 4 million tons per year when the First Five-Year Plan began in 1929. By 1939 steel output had reached 18 million tons per year, and after a setback during World War II it surged ahead to reach a level of 76 million tons per year in 1962. The Soviet heavy industrial establishment is second only to that of the United States. In terms of the industrial capacity available to meet the military needs of the government, the Soviet Union is virtually on a par with the United States. Here, then, are the decisive roots of Soviet Russia's present world influence: the ability of a totalitarian government, through the "command economy" of state ownership and planning, to channel the maximum proportion of the nation's effort and resources into the production of the industrial sinews of modern power.

A very different picture is seen in the areas of consumer goods, personal services, and agriculture. These fields have been consistently short-changed in the allocation of money and materials, and they above all others have suffered from the overcentralization of the Soviet economy, for these are the economic areas in which individual enterprise and initiative on a small scale are generally more effective. Shortages, high prices, and defective quality are chronic troubles for the Soviet consumer, although matters have improved greatly since Stalin's death.

About half of the Soviet population is still engaged in agriculture, a very high proportion for an industrial country and a reflection of the Russian legacy of rural overpopulation and backwardness. Soviet agriculture is basically limited, as we have seen, by the climatic conditions of much of the country and by the excess of rural population for whom there is so far nothing to do but remain on the farm (at the price of lower productivity by each peasant family). For the Soviet government the fundamental economic problem in agriculture has been to extract from the peasants a food surplus to feed the urban workers. Since the government has not been willing to invest in the production of consumer goods to trade with the peasants for their produce, the surplus has been taken in some form of tax or rent —just as it was taken through all the centuries of tsarist serfdom and landlordism. The institution for collecting this tax is the collective farm, a socialist ideal of economic organization applied in the Soviet Union with the manner and purposes of Russian despotism.

The Soviet collective farms (*kolkhozy*), which embrace some 90 per cent of all the peasants in the USSR, are cooperatives which hold their land from the state on a perpetual lease. Each of the 100 to 1,000 or more families who make up a *kolkhoz* has its own homestead and garden plot, usually in a village which long antedates the Revolution. Produce from the plot and from private animals is at the free disposal of the family, to consume or to sell in the open *kolkhoz* markets in the towns. The members of the family must also work on the collective fields, whose product is sold to the state under contract.

The state collects fees from the farm and pays artificially low prices for the farm's produce as a monopoly buyer. The farm's collective income is apportioned to meet the farm's expenses, the residue to be divided among the collective farmers in proportion to the time they have contributed and the nature of their skill. A chronic problem is the lack of incentive for the individual peasant to work hard on the collective fields. Because of this and the meagerness of investment in agricultural machinery and fertilizer, the state fails to get the desired total output, and most of the villages remain impoverished.

For special agricultural purposes—for research, for special crops such as cotton and sugar beets, and for developing grain production on the steppes of Central Asia—a different type of institution, the State Farm (*sovkhoz*) is used. This is a fully state-owned enterprise. The peasants work as hired laborers just as they would in a factory or on large-scale farms and plantations in non-Communist countries. The *sovkhozy* generally produce better and yield the peasants more, but their higher cost to the state will probably limit any expansion of this type of organization.

The governmental budget in the Soviet Union is very large because it includes the entire sum of new investment in industry as well as the ordinary expense of administration, public services, and military expenditure. The main device for raising money is the so-called turn-over tax. This represents the monopoly profit which the state-owned system of stores can earn through the difference between the cost of production and the price which consumers are willing to pay for commodities in short supply. The turnover tax is heavy on food and other items of mass consumption and bears most heavily on those least able to pay. Income and inheritance taxes are relatively low, and while there are none of the spectacularly high incomes which are possible under capitalism, those top-ranking administrators and intellectuals whom the state feels it necessary to reward can keep most of their income and live in ample comfort.

In theory, the Soviet Union is a classless society because the Communist regime has abolished private property in the means of production. Practically everyone is an employee of the state, but at widely different levels of skill, responsibility, remuneration, and status. In actuality, Soviet society is very highly stratified, with a marked consciousness of status. On the other hand, as in the United States, there are no very sharp lines between one class and another, and it is fairly easy for a talented individual to move up through the ranks. The main social strata are as follows: the upper class of high officials—Party, governmental and industrial—together with a few favored intellectuals (about 1 million families); the upper middle class of lower officials, engineers and scientists, and military officers (about 5 million families); the lower middle class of white-collar workers, teachers, and technicians (about 5 million families); the proletariat of manual workers in factories, mines, etc. (about 20 million families); and the peasants (about 25 million families).* The motive of social and economic advancement is a powerful one, and the Soviet government takes full advantage of salary and prestige incentives to get the maximum performance from all social groups.

Equality of the sexes has been a firm Communist principle since the Revolution, and the Soviet Union has outdistanced most other countries in the proportion of women in professional and managerial work. But equality has its negative aspects as well, in the heavy manual labor which proletarian and peasant women share. Family life is as normal as the circumstances of crowded housing and working mothers permit. The early Soviet condonement of free love and easy divorce has long since given way to official puritanism.

Viewed as a whole, the Soviet economic and social structure bears little relation to the Marxist ideal, aside from the negative fact that it excludes private capitalists. Soviet society is a complex, bureaucratic, hierarchical system in which everyone must work under almost military discipline, enjoying a free private life but little freedom on the job and none with regard to political affairs.

Soviet society is a peculiar combination of the ultimate bureaucratic logic of modern industrialism superimposed on the Russian tradition of statism and centralism. The Soviet state could be likened to a gigantic capitalist monopoly, in which everyone, high and low, is an employee. No class really rules; the upper class is no freer than the lower. As in the Russian Empire before the nineteenth century, society is in bondage to the state; every social institution is controlled, shaped, or created by the state; and the goals of the whole society are established autocratically at the top. The prevailing purpose in Soviet society is still, as it has been for centuries, the mobilization of the maximum economic and military power of the nation.

Soviet Thought and Culture

Both in principle and in practice, Soviet thought and culture are instruments to serve the purposes of the Communist Party. The principle, rooted in the political obsessions of the nineteenth-century Russian intelligentsia, is that of *partiinost*—partisanship or party spirit—rejecting independent standards of objectivity or aesthetic

* See Barrington Moore, *Soviet Politics: The Dilemma of Power*, pp. 280-283.

merit in favor of practical or propagandist service to the Party. Bureaucratic control is exercised through the centralized mass media of broadcasting, publishing, and education, and through Party control over every form of public assembly. Nothing can be said, printed, exhibited, or otherwise communicated publicly in the Soviet Union unless it has Party approval, and for this it must conform closely to the intellectual strictures of the official Marxist-Leninist doctrine as currently interpreted.

Marxism-Leninism is the official philosophy of the CPSU and the Soviet government. It is supposed to be a compound of the basic theories of Karl Marx and Friedrich Engels, updated and applied to Russia by Lenin. According to this doctrine, the advent of the Soviet regime was the first instance of an anticipated world-wide series of proletarian revolutions. These were to replace the bourgeoisie with the industrial workers as the ruling class, abolish capitalism, create a socialist economy, and then commence the transition to the ideal, classless, propertyless, moneyless, stateless society of pure communism. The Soviet regime under Khrushchev officially claims to be making the transition from socialism to communism, while the other Communist countries are said to be in various stages of building socialism.

Doctrine is important to the Soviet leaders as an instrument of totalitarian control over public thought and belief. Authority to interpret the meaning of doctrine rests in the hands of a very few at the top level of the Party. The Soviet leaders have from the start felt it necessary to couch their policies and decisions in ideological terms, but they have not let this prevent them from introducing every sort of expedient novelty in their practical policies, from inequality of wage payments to the condemnation of modern literature and the conclusion of alliances with capitalist governments. On the whole, ideology has not dictated policy; it has been reinterpreted after the fact to give theoretical justification to whatever practical policy may have been adopted.

Such practical and propagandist modification of doctrine is perhaps most graphically illustrated by the marriage of nationalistic and Marxist themes, accomplished by Stalin in the 1930s and still in effect. Recognizing the reality of national feeling and its power to further the interests of the state, the Soviet regime cultivates the mass sense of patriotism to the utmost. The regime has even suggested the superiority of the Russians over the other Soviet nationalities and has claimed a unique position for the Soviet Union in relation to other Marxist governments in the achievement of the Communist utopia.

Such use of Marxism-Leninism has involved both righteous self-deception on the part of the Communist leaders and stringent control over the public discussion of Marxism. Marxist theory—and the areas of political and social thought which it touches—is the subject on which the leadership can least tolerate any independent opinion or criticism. Once the Party under Stalin had embarked on the course of self-justification by manipulating doctrine, the maintenance of Party authority required the suppression of any thought that the Party might not in fact have a monopoly on truth. From this requirement have stemmed the Party's pervasive controls not only over political opinion but over ideas and cultural creations in every field whatsoever.

Party interference in Soviet cultural and intellectual life varies in direct proportion to the political implications of a subject. In political thought, sociology, and philosophy there is nothing save the crudities of Party propaganda. Economic thought allows for little more, although of late there has been some effort to appreciate Western computer techniques, investment calculations, and so on. Psychology is largely restricted to physiological studies. In the biological and physical sciences inquiry usually proceeds with a real respect for the truth, though in Stalin's time the Party went so far as to condemn as reactionary such fundamental scientific propositions as Einstein's theory of relativity and the Mendelian theory of genetics. Literature and the arts are subject to Party interference and censorship but necessarily involve an element of individual creativity. These cultural fields have enjoyed a little more leeway since the mid-1950s and have accordingly become what they were under the unreformed tsarism of the early and middle nineteenth century—the principal avenue for criticism and individual self-assertion in a society otherwise shackled by the dead hand of autocracy and bureaucracy. However, literary freedom still has narrow limits, exemplified by the suppression of Boris Pasternak's *Doctor Zhivago* and the repeated censure of popular young writers such as Yevgeny Yevtushenko.

Soviet Russia is still two nations, the intelligentsia and the toilers. The Soviet government has always been sensitive to this and has attacked the cleavage from both directions by uplifting the masses and holding the educated class down. The binding standard for art and literature is that it be understandable to the masses, and for 30 years or more all modernistic experimentalism has been taboo. On the other hand, the regime has worked assiduously to achieve mass education and universal literacy in a country that was half illiterate at the time of the Revolution.

Education is the one aspect of the Soviet system which has been acclaimed in the outside world almost without reservation. Its achievements in the realm of science and technological training are simply the fruit of a European-style selective secondary education system, plus the power of the Soviet regime to channel its best minds into the fields where they do the most good for the state. Universal compulsory education is now in force in the Soviet Union, but not everywhere is it available for the full eight years which is supposed to be the standard requirement. Academic secondary education (heavily intermixed with "polytechnical" shopwork) is elective and exists largely in urban areas. A majority of the youth go into trade schools or employment with supplementary vocational classes. The Soviet Union has wider access to secondary and higher education than does Western Europe, though not so wide as the American system. Soviet Russia seems to be moving in the American direction of mass secondary education but has nothing that approximates the American college.

Higher education in the Soviet Union, as in continental Europe, is entirely professional or specialized, corresponding to the American graduate school or professional school. Soviet universities and professional institutes now quantitatively exceed the American capacity to provide professional manpower, notably in the scientific and engineering fields. At the topmost level of scientific research there are some Soviet specialists equal to any in the world, but the numbers of the really competent people appear to be limited. Observers have noted that the best Soviet scholars and scientists are the very old, those trained before the Revolution, or the very young, who matured after the passing of Stalinism. The student, the scholar, and the expert are well rewarded, and education is the chief avenue to personal advancement in Soviet society.

The educated Russian is intellectually serious and far more interested in matters of theory or speculation than his American counterpart, which helps explain the Communist movement's concern for rigorous theoretical justification. Communist indoctrination has even familiarized the masses with theoretical concerns, though it has repelled most of the intellectuals with its boring crudeness. Soviet society probably contains a vast latent force for philosophical inquiry and aesthetic adventure, if the Communist Party should ever permit such developments.

One cultural tradition which persists despite official condemnation is religion. Soviet sources concede that half the population are still believers, and serious efforts to eradicate religion have not been at-

tempted since before World War II. The Russian Orthodox Church
—the national branch of the Greek Orthodox Church—is the traditional faith of most of the Great Russians, Byelorussians, Ukrainians,
and Georgians. It enjoys a distinctly favored position among the
Soviet religions, with its own elaborate organization headed by the
Patriarch of Moscow. The Orthodox Church is closely identified with
Russian nationalism and is a tool of public control and discipline
to encourage obedience to the Soviet state.

Other faiths in the Soviet Union are generally associated with the
national minorities—Judaism; the Roman Catholicism of Lithuania
and the western Ukraine; Lutheranism in Estonia and Latvia; the
independent Christian Church of Armenia; and the Moslems—some
30 million of them—in Azerbaijan, among the Volga Tatars, and in
the republics of Central Asia. Among the Russians there are a minority belonging to the sect of Old Believers, which split off from the
Orthodox Church in the seventeenth century. There are also numerous Protestant denominations (among them two million Baptists),
the product of German influence in the eighteenth century. The non-
Orthodox religions are much more likely to incur suspicion and repression by the Soviet state, either because they have strong international
ties (Catholics and Jews), resist modern ways (Moslems), or represent an escape from the disciplined society (Old Believers and the
Pentecostal Protestant sects, which have been growing rapidly). The
Jews in particular have borne the brunt of official hostility under
Khrushchev.

The Party's antireligious propaganda and the government's restrictions on religious education have curtailed active religious participation except among the peasants and old people. There are, however,
instances of personal philosophic or religious questing by some members of the intelligentsia. On balance, the Soviet masses are
probably being secularized about as fast as the masses in comparable
non-Communist industrial societies.

Apart from science and technology, the effect of Communist rule
on Soviet thought and culture has been to deaden or inhibit most
of the nation's vast potential for intellectual creativity. A great possible Russian contribution to modern world thought, heralded by
Russia's leadership in intellectual and artistic modernism in the first
quarter of this century—has been lost or so far withheld. In science
Soviet work has forged ahead impressively, if unevenly, in a wide
range of specialties, and Russian has become the world's second scientific language, next to English. As in economics, so in thought and
education, the pressure of the totalitarian state has directed produc-

tivity into the service of the state and its industrial, military, and propagandist concerns.

The Nature of the Soviet System

A major obstacle in assessing the realities of Soviet Russia is the ideological myth of Marxism-Leninism which holds that the Communist regime in Russia is something entirely new. All too often observers of Soviet affairs forget that historically, culturally, demographically, and geographically the USSR is still the old Russian Empire, even though it has assumed a new and very different political form. The USSR is still the great world power, Russia, though it is a Russia that has gone through a unique series of violent experiences in recent decades—the experience of accelerated westernization and industrialization, the experience of a great social revolution, and the experience of totalitarian rule. The outcome is a combination of native traits and Western techniques that might be described as a system of militaristic industrialism.

Marxist-Leninist theory has a peculiar and little understood role in this system. It is, literally, the official faith, furnishing the liturgical language for what amounts to a secular theocracy. The theory is not the open scientific hypothesis its originator intended it to be, nor a plan of action, but rather a verbal source for self-righteous rationalization of action on the part of the Communist leadership. This has permitted a vast evolution in the policies and forms of the Communist system under the veil of an ostensibly unchanging doctrine. Where a second Communist power has arisen—in China—which is able to determine its own policies and revise the doctrine in its own way, the result is a split and the exchange of mutual accusations of anti-Marxist heresy by the Soviet and Chinese leaders. Official Communist theory has not guided the evolution of the Soviet Union, nor can it explain that evolution. Ideological blinders prevent the Soviet authorities from understanding their own society as well as foreign observers can.

Soviet Russia is a manifestation of the whole of Russian history. It demonstrates the primacy and endurance of the nation as an historical category, and the force of nationalism—in whatever terms it is expressed—as the criterion for governmental decision and as a major emotional bond in society. Nationalism may not be eternal, and it has declined in Western Europe after a 40-year orgy, but for Soviet Russia no less than for the United States and for the newly independent states of Asia and Africa, nationalism is still the dominant value by which the policy of government is set.

TWO

THE RUSSIAN PAST

Russia, like any country or human institution, is a product
of its past, but it has been shaped and colored by that past in a
unique way. From the international standpoint, Russia was long
denied the opportunity to become a national state. Once that status
was achieved, Russia quickly expanded into a multinational empire,
often overextending itself militarily. Russia achieved an autocracy far
beyond the strength and pervasiveness of most others. Socially and
economically, Russia was marked by its failure to progress except
under pressure by the government or under foreign influence. Culturally and intellectually, Russia was never able to achieve a firm
sense of identity or accomplishment in the shadow of superior foreign
civilizations. In the chapter that follows we will explore each of
these aspects of the Russian heritage. In conclusion, we will try to
assess the ways in which these historical peculiarities have appeared
again to shape the nature of Soviet Russia today.

The Rise of the Russian Nation

Russia has never been a secure national unit. The earliest Russian
governments of medieval times were plagued by internal disunity and
nomad invasions, while Russia's expansion in modern times quickly
encompassed a host of non-Russian peoples. Warfare has always been
the Russian government's uppermost concern. Russia was born, grew,
and lived in struggle, grimly endured by the masses, pursued as a self-
justifying end by their rulers. A weak and impoverished society was
made—and remains—the unwilling tool of one of history's most
spectacular ascents to greatness.

Russian history proper begins comparatively late in the annals of
civilization with the establishment of a number of city-state principalities in the ninth century A.D. in what is now the western part of
European Russia. The nomadic cultures of the Black Sea coast and
the civilizations of Transcaucasia reaching back to 2000 B.C. do not

belong to Russian history proper so much as to the history of societies later conquered and assimilated by Russia. Russia's own beginnings are disputed. Traditional scholars ascribe to the Varangians (Norsemen) the country's first enduring political organization, while Soviet historians insist that it was the work of the Slavic tribes. In any event, by 900 A.D. western Russia was organized into some dozen principalities, each dependent on a trading town (of which the most illustrious were Novgorod and Kiev). The princes all claimed descent from the legendary Viking Riurik, who, according to the medieval chronicles, was invited to rule the town of Novgorod and create an effective government.

The subjects of these princes were Slavic-speaking tribesmen who had but recently emerged from seminomadic barbarism into the settled life of town and village. There was as yet no clear differentiation into the present Great Russian, Byelorussian, and Ukrainian languages and nationalities. Kiev, thanks to its location and the exploits of its princes, soon became the economic, cultural, and political center of the Russian principalities. The entire epoch of Russian history up to the Mongol conquest in the thirteenth century is known as the Kievan period. Under the remarkable Prince Sviatoslav (962-972), Kievan military expeditions terrorized the Byzantine Empire, cemented Kiev's hegemony over the other Russian states, and dominated the entire Black Sea basin.

Inspired by the cultural achievements of Constantinople, the Kievans under Prince Vladimir (980-1015) received the Orthodox Christian faith of the Byzantines and eventually made it the state religion of all the Russian principalities. The conversion can be viewed as the symbolic act of accession to civilization—but to the civilization of the Greek Orthodox East, not of the Roman Catholic West.

Until the eighteenth century Russia remained walled off from Western Europe and from the cultural achievements of medieval and early modern times which are the common heritage of every country from Portugal to Poland and from Norway to Italy, together with their overseas settlements in the Americas. The Russian branch of the Orthodox Church, with its liturgy and scriptures written in the old Slavic dialect known as Church Slavonic, became a distinctly Russian institution and a major factor in the survival of Russian national consciousness through the ensuing centuries of disorder and conquest.

Kiev reached its height in the eleventh century during the long and able rule of Prince Yaroslav the Wise (1019-1054). After he died the reassertion of princely localism and the resumption of nomad attacks began to weaken the Kievan realm. Population and political power shifted toward the frontier in the northeast—the central part of present-day European Russia—where new and vigorous principalities arose. In 1169 Prince Andrei Bogolubsky of Vladimir (some 100 miles east of the present location of Moscow) dramatized the shift by conquering Kiev, moving the head of the Russian Church (the Metropolitan) from Kiev to Vladimir and proclaiming Vladimir as the chief Russian state with himself as Grand Prince.

Internecine warfare between princely brothers and cousins continued to weaken the Russian states and made them easy prey to the last and mightiest of the Central Asian nomadic invasions in the 1220s and 1230s. Between 1237 and 1240 the Mongols and their Tatar (Turkish-speaking) allies under Batu Khan, grandson of Genghis Khan, conquered the whole of Russia. For the next two centuries the Russians remained under Mongol suzerainty, though the native Russian princes were allowed to keep their thrones as Mongol puppets by serving as tax collectors for their conquerors.

The Mongol conquest was a devastating blow to the development of civilization in Russia. Urban life and trade were badly damaged, warfare and revolts bled the nation, and the cultural link to Constantinople was severed. Russia entered the modern world in the seventeenth century with a culture comparable to the early medieval period in Western Europe.

The period of Mongol overlordship witnessed the rise of the new principality of Moscow, which was ultimately to unite the whole of Russia. Moscow came to prominence under Prince Ivan I, "Moneybags" (1325-1341), who secured Mongol recognition as their chief Russian agent. The Metropolitan of the Church and the title "Grand Prince of Vladimir" were transferred to Moscow. With this advantage Moscow then waged a century of successful wars against rival principalities and simultaneously organized Russian resistance against the Mongols. The victory of Moscow's Prince Dmitri Donskoi in the battle of Kulikovo (1380) was the turning point that signaled the waning power of the Mongols and Tatars and the growing autonomy of the Russian states.

The great transformation in the history of Moscow and of Russia came with the reign of Ivan III, the Great (1462-1505). Starting with what was already the largest of all the Russian principalities, Ivan proceeded to annex most of the neighboring Russian states by conquest or diplomacy. By the close of his reign he had created a centralized Russian national state encompassing all of what is now northern and central European Russia, in place of the multitude of warring principalities which had maintained their separate existence ever since the founding of Kiev. The authority of the new state was strengthened by Ivan's official repudiation of Mongol-Tatar overlordship in 1480, and later on by the doctrine of the Third Rome, according to which Moscow had succeeded Rome and Constantinople as the seat of the supreme Christian ruler.

Meanwhile, other parts of Russia—the west and northwest, including Kiev—had been taken from the Mongols not by Moscow but by the rising Grand Duchy of Lithuania. These regions remained under Lithuanian and then Polish rule, separate from Russia and closer to Western influence, until the seventeenth and eighteenth centuries, and the local language evolved into modern Ukrainian and Byelorussian.

Russia's attainment of national statehood was but a short-lived prelude to a long drama of imperial expansion. Ivan the Great's grandson, Ivan IV, the Terrible (1533-1584), took the field both eastward and westward. The Poles and Swedes threw him back from the shores of the Baltic, but to the east he vanquished the Tatars of the Volga region and made them subjects of the Russian Tsar ("Caesar," as Ivan and his successors styled themselves). Ivan's victories cleared the path for the exploration of Siberia, and bands of Russian frontiersmen and Cossacks made their way further eastward year by year until in 1637 they reached the Pacific Ocean and claimed the whole northern third of Asia for the Russian crown.

From the sixteenth century to the twentieth the Russian drive to expand continued without restriction by any sense of "natural" limits to the empire. Only the military power of determined neighbors curbed Russian ambitions. In the seventeenth and eighteenth centuries Russia turned westward and southwestward against three old but declining powers: the Poles, then the Swedes, then the Turks, who yielded in turn to the Russian advance. By the close of the eighteenth century the Russians commanded their adjacent coasts on the Baltic and the Black Sea and had penetrated far enough into East-Central Europe to bring almost all the East Slavs—Ukrainians and Byelorussians, together with the Great Russians—last under the rule of the Tsar.

Russia emerged into the international community of the European powers in the reign of Peter I, the Great (1682-1725). It was Peter who won for his country a place in the ranks of the great powers by his victory over Sweden in the Great Northern War of 1700-1721 and by the resulting annexation of the East Baltic coast (including the site of the new Russian capital of St. Petersburg). These gains brought under Russian rule the ancestors of the present-day Estonians and Latvians, together with the German upper class of these territories (the "Baltic Barons"), who played a major role in westernizing the Russian government during the next century. Peter himself followed a deliberate policy of westernization, especially in military affairs and education. Peter's steps were not without precedent, but his reign was the true watershed between a Russia living in near isolation and a Russia ready to enter—if uneasily—into Western civilization.

In the decades following Peter's reign Russia, despite the instability of the throne itself, was a regular participant in Europe's diplomacy, alliances, and wars. Under Catherine II, the Great (1762-1796), Russian forces took the Crimea and the northern coast of the Black Sea from the Turkish Empire. To the west, Catherine tried to reduce the once proud kingdom of Poland to the status of a Russian satellite by putting her ex-lover Stanislas Poniatowski on the Polish throne, but Austrian and Prussian resistance forced her to settle for three successive partitions of Poland in 1772, 1793, and 1795. These gave Russia most of the non-Polish-speaking population of Poland—the Lithuanians, the Byelorussians, and most of the Ukrainians.

During the Napoleonic Wars Russia's international influence reached an unprecedented height thanks to the Russian role in checking the expansion of the Revolutionary French Empire. In 1807 Alexander I (1801-1825) made a truce with Napoleon (often compared to the Stalin-Hitler pact of 1939) that divided Europe into two great spheres of influence, French and Russian. Russia utilized this opportunity to conquer Finland from Sweden in 1809, to annex Turkey's Rumanian province of Bessarabia in 1812, and to pursue the conquest of Transcaucasia from Turkey and Persia. Napoleon's ill-fated invasion of Russia in 1812, like Hitler's in 1941, resulted in the total defeat of the invaders, and an important place for Russia in the councils of Europe.

At the Congress of Vienna in 1814 and 1815 Alexander I successfully pressed upon Europe his schemes of alliance—the Quadruple Alliance and the Holy Alliance—to curb France in particular and revolution in general. For the next 40 years Russia was the feared and hated leader of Europe's conservative bloc. Aided by Austria and Prussia the Tsars made a determined effort to suppress all forms of liberal protest and national revolt wherever in Europe such movements arose from the legacy of the French Revolution.

Russia's direct share of the spoils after the Napoleonic Wars was the Congress Kingdom of Poland, a revived Polish state formed out of the Austrian and Prussian share of the partitions and placed incongruously under Russia's Alexander I as the constitutional king of Poland. This Polish-speaking, Roman Catholic heart of the old Polish state proved to be a far more indigestible conquest than any of Russia's previous acquisitions. The Poles violently though vainly rebelled in 1830 and again in 1863 and kept their national tradition vigorously alive through another half-century of tsarist oppression, not to mention German occupation and Communist domination in recent times.

Russia made no further effort to expand westward after 1815 because in that direction lay the unassailable and, moreover, friendly powers of Prussia and Austria. Toward the south it was another matter, and the diplomatic history of the nineteenth century is crammed with the record of crises brought about by Russian efforts to penetrate the decaying Turkish Empire and to bring the Balkan Peninsula into the Russian political orbit. The ideological rationale of this drive was the doctrine of Pan-Slavism, according to which it was Russia's mission to liberate all "brother" Slavs of the Balkans and bring them into a new federation under Russian leadership. The territorial objectives of these Pan-Slav schemes were remarkably similar to the area occupied by the bloc of Communist satellites which the Soviet Union established in Eastern Europe after 1945.

Russia fought Turkey three more times in the nineteenth century, only to have her ambitions curbed each time by the intervention of other European powers. To establish a foothold in the Turkish Empire, Russia aided the rebelling Greek nationalists in 1828. Britain, France, and the Italian kingdom of Piedmont-Sardinia came to Turkey's aid in the Crimean War of 1854-1856. Russia's victories over the Turks in 1876-1877 provoked the Congress of Berlin and a successful effort by Britain and Austria to make Russia relinquish her conquests. In the end Russia had only an alliance with the Balkan kingdom of Serbia and the deep grudge of frustrated imperialist ambition. Here, as it turned out, lay the tinder that set off the great war of 1914-1918 and brought about the ruin of the tsarist regime.

Meanwhile, Russia extended her power eastward. In the 1820s Russian expeditions into the Central Asian steppes and desert subdued the nomads and conquered the small Moslem Turkish principalities to the north of Persia and Afghanistan. By the 1880s Russia had arrived at its present Middle Eastern border, though not without

arousing intense British hostility. Russia would no doubt have con-
tinued south to the Indian Ocean had not the British propped up
Persia and Afghanistan as buffer states to protect their empire in
India.

On the Pacific coast Russia succeeded in moving the border south-
ward to the Amur River and Vladivostok in the 1850s and 1860s, at
the expense of the revolt-torn Chinese Empire. In the 1890s Russia
attempted to make China's northeastern province of Manchuria and
the kingdom of Korea into satellites. In the Far East, as in Europe,
the Balkans, and Central Asia, Russian expansion was stopped only
by the presence of other major powers: this time by the newly
westernized Japanese Empire, a natural rival of Russia for the spoils
of the crumbling Chinese Empire. Russian moves into Korea and
the Yellow Sea base of Port Arthur led to a Japanese attack and the
Russo-Japanese War of 1904-1905. Quick Japanese victories on sea
and land put a stop to further Russian expansion in Asia until after
World War II.

Despite the checks which other powerful countries had administered to Russian ambitions during the preceding half-century, Russia
on the eve of World War I and the Revolution was still a major
imperial power. Russia's boundaries were actually more extensive than
the present territory of the Soviet Union, except in the Far East,
where the USSR has regained South Sakhalin and the Kurile Islands.
On the other hand, Russia had lagged behind Britain, France, and
Germany, not to mention the United States and Japan, in industrial
development. A full-scale industrial revolution had commenced in
Russia only in the 1880s and 1890s, and politically and socially even
more than economically Russia had lost ground to the dynamic West.
It was under these conditions of tension and frustration that Russia
joined the great alliance of the French and British against the Germans and Austrians and became inextricably involved in the tangled
politics of the Balkans, thereby contributing to the outbreak of
"total war" in August 1914.

The Russian Autocracy

Soviet totalitarianism is—or was until it began to be exported after
World War II—a unique system of political and social organization.
Russia's political and social structure under the tsars was also unique.
Autocracy—its nature and its behavior—is the overwhelming theme
of the political history of Russia.

Russian historians have long recognized the peculiarities of Russia's
political life, in particular the "overgrowth" of the state stressed by

the so-called statist school of Russian historical writing in the nine-teenth century. While the West experienced its own period of ab-solute monarchy in the early modern period, the Muscovite absolute monarchy was in every respect more absolute. It was less subject to the restraints of representative or judicial bodies, more thoroughly centralized, and unhampered by separate local authorities. Its author-ity was challenged by fewer nonpolitical powers and privileges such as those of the churches or of propertied social groups. It exerted far more control over nonpolitical matters than was ever the case in the West. While the authority of the state had weakened in the decades just prior to the Revolution, it left its mark imprinted in the habits of both the rulers and the ruled and in the unspoken premises with which a new company of rulers came to power in 1917.

Until the Mongol conquest Russian political experience did not differ much from that of Western and Central Europe. Organized government came into being in Russia, as in Western Europe, as an extension and formal territorial solidification of earlier tribal allegiances. By about 900 A.D. most of what is now western Russia from Novgorod to Kiev was divided among the numerous autono-mous princes of the so-called Riurik dynasty.

This early Russian political system might be called a form of feudalism, if feudalism is understood loosely enough to allow for the differences among its Russian, West European, and other forms. The Russian princes were linked in a sort of family confederation under their principal member, the Grand Prince of Kiev. Each prince was served by a band of warriors who were rewarded with land and became landowning aristocrats called boyars. Each princi-pality was governed from a trading town, where the town council (*veche*) shared certain powers with the prince and with the council of boyars.

Princely authority in Kievan Russia was regarded as the personal property of the ruling family, and (as in Merovingian Gaul) princi-palities were partitioned among all the sons of a deceased ruler. Theoretically, the various related princes had the right to move to larger towns and ultimately to Kiev on the basis of seniority, but in practice such claims, like the partition of principalities among brothers, were the subject of chronic military strife among the princes. Russia suffered from such internal warfare even more than Western Europe in the darkest days of feudalism, and was exhausted and disorganized when the Mongols came to conquer.

There were certain regional differences among the early Russian principalities. To the west and southwest of Kiev, the aristocracy predominated in government as it then did in most of Europe to the west. In the northwest, Novgorod and its sister city of Pskov became merchant republics controlled by the town assemblies, like the medieval city-states of Italy and Germany. To the northeast, the frontier of new migration and settlement where security was at a premium, princely authority prevailed. In explanation of these differences, the historian Paul Miliukov has suggested that the development of a stable nobility in western Russia prior to the emergence of a strong princely government on the Byzantine model allowed the continuance of aristocratic power and independence in that region, whereas the reverse situation in northeastern Russia gave the princely power a head start which was never effectively challenged. The more autocratic northeastern region was the cradle of the later Russian Empire, and therefore the more decisive influence in Russian history.

The effect of the Mongol conquest on Russia's political development has been argued by Russian historians for generations. The negative consequences are clear: human losses in combat, destruction of towns or of the institutions of urban self-government, cultural isolation, and the economic burden of taxes and tribute for the Mongols. The Mongols did not, however, destroy the political existence of the Russian principalities.

From their capital at Sarai on the lower Volga the Mongols themselves ruled the southern steppes, but the princes of what had been Kievan Russia were employed in a system of indirect rule. As policemen, tax collectors, and military recruiting agents for the Mongols, the Russian princes probably enjoyed more direct authority over their own subjects than they had ever had before. Some scholars contend that the princes also benefited from new techniques and theories of government borrowed from the Mongols: the use of direct taxation, conditional land grants as a form of military salary, and the notion of unlimited power in the person of the prince. An extreme version of this interpretation is the theory of oriental despotism advanced by Karl Wittfogel, stressing the bureaucratic absolutism of the "agro-managerial society," which supposedly originated in China and the Middle East to superintend irrigation works and was carried into Eastern Europe through the despotic practices of the Byzantines and the Mongols. Whatever its sources, the tradition of imperial absolutism was continued and enhanced by Prince Ivan the Great, along with the Byzantine practice of close subordination of the Church to the state.

For more than a century following Ivan III's work of national consolidation, Muscovy was torn by violent struggles between the prince and the families of the upper nobility who strove to retain their influence in the central government. These nobles had long participated in the Boyar Duma, or council, whose advice the prince was supposed to consider. To this was added in the mid-sixteenth century a broader advisory institution called the Zemsky Sobor, or assembly of the land, with representatives of the towns and free peasants as well as of the upper and lower nobility. Unlike the contemporary development of parliamentary institutions in many Western countries, however, the Zemsky Sobor never achieved more than advisory power, and after the middle of the seventeenth century it ceased to be used at all.

The great crisis in the contest between autocracy and aristocracy began in the second half of the reign of Ivan the Terrible. Ivan, at his coronation in 1547 at the age of 16, took the title of Tsar, or Caesar. In the 1560s, plagued by treason, or suspicion of treason, among his boyars, Ivan set up a new governmental administration, the *oprichnina*, under his personal control and undertook a physical purge of the noble families. Ivan killed his own eldest son and heir, leaving the crown to his incompetent second son, Fyodor (1584-1598). Ivan's autocratic rule was continued by the brother-in-law of Fyodor, Boris Godunov, who was the power behind the throne until 1598 and then claimed the throne for himself. This break in the legitimate succession was the signal for rebellion by the nobility.

Godunov's reign produced a decade of revolutionary turmoil, the so-called time of troubles from 1604 to 1613. Russia was torn by noble plots, peasant uprisings, and outside intervention by the Poles and Swedes. Half a dozen contenders struggled for the throne, until in 1612-1613 a movement of national resistance against the Poles led to the election of Mikhail Romanov as Tsar by the Zemsky Sobor. This period of tumult might be thought to have weakened autocracy in favor of the nobility or the representative institutions, but its actual effect, paradoxically, was to exhaust the forces of opposition and leave the principle of absolute monarchy unchallenged.

Still more surprising in the history of the Russian autocracy is the stability and power of the monarchy itself as an institution, despite the personal weakness of individual monarchs (especially in the seventeenth century) and disorders in the succession from one monarch to the next. From 1682 to 1917 every Russian monarch either gained or lost the throne under circumstances of revolutionary violence. The explanation may be found in the unbroken development since Kievan times of central political authority at the expense of other social institutions. No class save the upper nobility had the power to resist the monarchy, and they were undermined by the growth of a service nobility, or gentry (*pomeshchiki*), who held land only as officers of the crown and therefore usually backed the central authority. Institutions such as the Church and the Zemsky Sobor sooner or later allowed themselves to become tools of the monarchy.

To be sure, revolt was endemic at many levels of Russian society: the noble families, the guards regiments, the Moscow mob, the Cossacks, the serfs. Great peasant rebellions flared in the seventeenth and eighteenth centuries. But no movement of resistance had the organization or staying power to succeed, except the military plots that seized the throne itself and continued the old system with new personnel. Many writers have noted the "apathy-or-revolt" pattern in Russian history, and what we might term the Russians' "readiness to be ruled," even though unhappily. In the Soviet experience the same phenomenon seems to have reappeared: autocracy is the natural way to get things done, and the people can only accept the irresistible.

The westernization of the reign of Peter the Great produced great differences in policy and some in form, but little in the real structure of power. Peter reorganized and renamed his departments of central and local government in imitation of his Swedish enemies. He pursued systematically the mercantilist encouragement of trade and industry as it was practiced in the West. Purges and promotions were "revolutionary," in injecting a temporary social mobility into Russia's class structure. The cultural and educational transformation of the upper class set in motion by Peter's policies had far-reaching consequences. But in the deepest political sense Peter's westernization was self-negating because it was so un-Western in method. Serf and noble alike were bound to the state in deeper bondage than ever.

Peter's death in 1725 signaled the beginning of an era of palace revolutions. During nearly 40 years of dynastic chaos strong women, foreign adventurers, military leaders, and noble factions struggled to possess the throne or the place of influence behind it. There was even a brief attempt to curb the autocracy itself when the highest and most conservative nobility tried to impose the so-called Conditions on Peter's niece Anna upon her accession to the throne in 1730. A military coup supported by the lower gentry quickly put an end to these limitations on the power of the throne, and during the remainder of the eighteenth century the Russian autocracy grew ever stronger through the reigns of three domineering empresses: Anna (1730-1740), Peter's daughter Elizabeth (1741-1762), and his German granddaughter-in-law Catherine the Great.

A signal development of the mid-eighteenth century was the emancipation of the nobility from compulsory state service. This was the work of Catherine's insane but ideologically enlightened husband, Peter III, who apparently planned to follow through with a corresponding emancipation of the peasants. Before he could do so he was murdered in a palace revolution sponsored by his wife. Catherine, in line with her own theoretical affinity for the Age of Enlightenment, experimented with schemes of representation and self-government for the nobility, but these came to nought. By the end of the eighteenth century the Russian nobility had become a powerless and functionless but privileged class of landowners, additionally serving as the nearly exclusive recruiting ground for the higher bureaucracy and the officer corps.

Catherine's superficial experiments with enlightened despotism came to an end upon the outbreak of the French Revolution in 1789. The repressiveness of the last years of her reign continued under her insanely capricious son, Paul (1796-1801). Paul was assassinated in the last of the successful palace revolutions, which elevated his son Alexander I to the throne and ushered in another superficial and unfruitful period of reform. Alexander even had his chief minister, Mikhail Speransky, draw up a proposal for representative constitutional government, but he lost sight of the scheme in his struggle with Napoleon and became a mystic and a reactionary in the years following the peace of 1815.

Alexander's reign, with its unfulfilled promises and disappointments of reform, witnessed the momentous parting of the ways between the Russian government and the westernized, educated upper class. Under the influence of Western example, the more enlightened of the gentry demanded reform. Discouragement and repression led some of the liberal army officers to form conspiratorial societies, and in 1825 these conspirators saw their chance to act.

When Alexander died in November 1825 (if he did die then— there are hints that he faked death and retired to Siberia as a hermit), the next in line to the throne was his liberal brother Constantine, then vice-regent in the constitutional kingdom of Poland. Constantine had secretly foresworn his right to the throne, which reverted to the youngest brother, Nicholas, a militaristic reactionary. The reformers attempted a military coup in December 1825, in favor of "Constantine and Constitution." The leaders of these

"Decembrists" bungled, and the revolt was crushed. Nicholas came to power with the confirmed determination to suppress every manifestation of liberal opinion in his realm.

The name of Nicholas I, the Iron Tsar, is a watchword for bureaucratic arbitrariness and obscurantist police methods. The gulf between the government and the enlightened gentry, the intelligentsia, became deep, permanent, and perhaps unbridgeable. Nevertheless, these conditions did not prevent Russia from experiencing one of the most striking outbursts of literary creativity that any country has ever displayed—the golden age of Russian literature, from Pushkin to Tolstoy and Dostoevsky. In the period of Nicholas I occurred the crystallization of the main currents of political and philosophical speculation which were to guide the revolutionary agitation and upheaval in Russia over the next three quarters of a century.

Nicholas I died in 1855 in the midst of the humiliating Crimean War, and with him died the last assurances that the Russian monarchy and Russian society could defy modernity and preserve all their old institutions intact. The ancient foundation of Russian society, serfdom, was left without defenders, and the new Tsar Alexander II made its abolition his first objective. The serfs were emancipated by imperial decree in 1861, thus ending hereditary human bondage in Russia just two years before the same was accomplished in the United States of America.

Alexander II followed up the Emancipation with a number of palliative modernizing measures, the Great Reforms. Representative local governments were established in the provinces and cities—though they could not infringe on the autocracy's exercise of police power. A modern judicial system with jury trial was established—though it did not extend to political crimes. Controls over the expression of opinion in the universities and the press were relaxed—though not enough to make free opposition a matter of right.

All of Alexander's reforms, the Emancipation included, were only halfway measures. The principle of absolute monarchy was never questioned. Far from satisfying the desires of the intellectual opposition, the reforms only whetted their appetite for change. Ironically, the history of continuous conspiratorial revolutionary activity in Russia dates from this very time.

It is still an open question whether, if Alexander II had moved faster or lived longer, the gulf between government and opposition could have been narrowed. The actual outcome was entirely the opposite, for the only successful reformer among Russia's tsars fell victim to a revolutionary's bomb in 1881. Alexander's son and heir,

Alexander III, came to the throne in a spirit of unrelenting absolutism reminiscent of Nicholas I, while ever wider circles of opposition saw the country's only hope in the violent overthrow of the monarchy. Nicholas II, when he succeeded his father in 1894, represented no change in the backward-looking attitude of the throne, except that he was personally incompetent. Russia's Louis XV had been succeeded by its Louis XVI. The immovable object of autocracy was confronted by the irresistible force of modernity, and a revolutionary crisis was then only a matter of time.

Backwardness and Bondage in Russian Society

To explain the unusual scope of autocratic power in Russia, it is necessary to look to the weaknesses in other aspects of society that permitted such political hypertrophy. Russian society throughout most of its history was depressed by the backwardness of its economy and hemmed in by legal encumbrances, so that no force could effectively challenge the pre-eminence of the autocracy. Quite the contrary: the government usually had to take action to correct or compensate for the economic and cultural weaknesses of Russian society.

Russia's material and cultural poverty goes back to the very beginnings of its history. Civilization came to Russia as a foreign import, sponsored mainly by the country's political (i.e., military) leaders. From the start, Russia's was a peripheral civilization, never thoroughly accepted by the people nor grounded in native creativity. Considering the rigors of climate in the era BCH—Before Central Heating—the very existence of civilization in Russia is something of an historical miracle. No other civilized society has arisen under such harsh conditions of winter climate.

Kievan society initiated the pattern of political leadership in social development. Trade was at first primarily a princely venture. The towns were the seats of princely authority. A noble class took shape and received land on the basis of service to the prince. The Christian Church was imported for princely prestige.

The vast majority of Kievans were seminomadic agriculturists who moved about as legally free men, paying some form of rent or service to each warrior in whose forests they cleared a patch to till. Kiev had slavery, chiefly in the towns, but it was hardly extensive enough to justify the claims of the earlier Marxist historians that Kiev was a form of the "slave-holding ancient society."

The Mongol invasion caused commercial retrogression and some two centuries of stagnation in Russian society. Physically and mentally, the Russian peasant of A.D. 1500 lived as crudely as the European peasant of A.D. 500; and the percentage of nonpeasants, with higher living standards, was probably just as small as in Europe 1000 years before. Under these circumstances the relatively advanced political organ of Muscovy established its enduring pre-eminence.

The princes of the Muscovite era were responsible for two key social developments in Russian history. They built up a service nobility of lesser gentry, who received conditional grants of land and in return sided with the autocracy against the higher boyars enjoying hereditary property rights. Through the sixteenth and seventeenth centuries the service nobility grew steadily larger and the privileges of the higher nobility steadily less distinct, until the two categories were finally merged by Peter the Great into an unconditionally duty-bound official class of state servants.

Serfdom was also promoted by the Russian government. It is striking that most of the peasants of undercivilized Russia had avoided bondage during the very era of chaos when the peasants of the Western world were forced into personal dependence on their lords. By 1500 serfdom had nearly disappeared in England, France and Italy; it was nearing its height in Germany, the Hapsburg domains, and Poland; but it was only beginning to take hold in Russia. The contrast is remarkable between the serfdom of the West that arose because the state was too weak to keep order and the serfdom of the East that arose because the state was strong enough to bind the peasants to the soil of the crown's noble servitors.

Government, as many Russian historians have stressed, was not the only force promoting serfdom in Russia. In particular, there were the debt obligations of the peasants to their landlords. Environment was also a factor, in a curious reversal of the frontier-freedom thesis. With plenty of land available, especially after Ivan IV's victories over the Tatars, the problem for the Russian landlord was to keep his peasants working and paying taxes on his own lands and to prevent them from fleeing to the service of some more lenient lord in the new frontier territory. Peasant movement also created a problem for the state in the enforcement of tax obligations and in the maintenance of a stable supply of peasant labor to support the service nobility. The result was a series of imperial decrees of the late sixteenth and early seventeenth centuries which restricted the right of peasant movement. These restrictions culminated in the law code of 1649 which made the bondage of the peasants complete, permanent, and hereditary.

Russia's era of westernization in the eighteenth century witnessed the depression of the serfs into a condition of veritable slavery. Peter the Great contributed to this by removing the legal distinction between serfs and slaves and by decreeing what amounted to a property tax paid by landholders on their serfs. Peter also extended serfdom by granting large tracts of state-owned land (including the peasants thereon, who were serfs of the state) to his favorites or to business entrepreneurs. In this unique system of subsidy the entrepreneur put these serfs to work as slave labor in building and operating mining or manufacturing establishments, whose output was then sold back to the government at a good profit.

For the nobility no less than for the peasants, the period of the late seventeenth and early eighteenth centuries had been a time of stricter servitude. Modernization was begun with the abolition of family rights of precedence in government offices (*mestnichestvo*) and the introduction by Peter of the bureaucratic Table of Ranks. Peter's reign, like that of Ivan the Terrible, was a time of the career open to talents; the old nobility was purged and expanded with the automatic ennobling of the Tsar's loyal officials, whatever their personal origins.

After Peter's death the social lines in Russia were hardened again by hereditary privilege, while the service obligations of the nobility progressively diminished. By the end of the eighteenth century the Russian nobility were personally free and lived on the revenues of what had become private property in land and serfs. These private holdings were increased by the practice of the eighteenth-century empresses of granting vast tracts to their court favorites, particularly after Catherine the Great secularized the Church lands. Somewhat less than half of the peasants remained state serfs, with some rights, but the majority on private estates became purely private chattels. Bloody peasant uprisings were common, and in 1773-1775 the entire Volga basin was swept by the serf and Cossack rebellion led by Pugachov. Nevertheless, the government, with its vastly superior organization and resources, was able to crush all resistance.

Peter's reforms and mercantilist subsidies had raised Russia almost to the European level of technology and production, if not of social organization and humaneness, but new trends in the European economy in the late eighteenth century soon left Russia behind again. The Industrial Revolution—really the onset of an industrial and technological *evolution* that still has not slackened—was beginning to transform the earth and man alike. As part of this evolution the West witnessed revolutionary new developments in machine technology and mechanical productivity, the growth of the factory system

and industrial capitalism, urbanization and the rise of a restive proletariat, political upheavals of liberalism and democracy, and an
accompanying intellectual and scientific ferment that offered every
sort of justification for and criticism of the new society.

All these developments passed Russia by for nearly a hundred
years. Until the 1880s and 1890s Russia remained overwhelmingly
rural and agrarian, politically unyielding, socially rigid. Then, in the
last years of the century, as though a dam had burst, the foundations
of the old order in Russia were inundated by a flood tide of westernization, modernization, and industrialization.

A dam literally had burst, if we can accept the argument of many
historians that it was the institution of serfdom that prevented the
modernization of Russian society and economy. The growing commercialization of the country as a whole diminished the interest of
the nobility in maintaining serfdom. Equally effective, however, were
the criticisms by the intellectuals and the mounting frequency of
peasant revolts that prompted Alexander II to announce the in-
evitability of emancipation, with the remark, "It would be much
better for this to come from above than from below."

The actual terms of the Emancipation were satisfactory to no one.
It was the commendable position of the government that emancipation should be accompanied by a distribution of land, wherein the
peasants would pay compensation to the landlords over half a
century. Actually, only about half the landlords' land went to the
peasants, while the required payments were exorbitant. In effect,
the serfs were being required to ransom their persons, and this kept
them in economic if not legal bondage.

Even the personal freedom granted to the serfs was strictly limited.
Special laws, punishments, and travel restrictions still applied to
the peasants as a legally inferior class. The peasant remained under
the jurisdiction of his village commune, which now exercised more
power than ever. The villagers in each commune were jointly responsible for the payment of taxes. In the old Muscovite lands the
commune itself owned the land and continued the traditional practice of redividing the land among its member families in accordance
with family size from generation to generation. This communal land
tenure led the nineteenth-century Russian intellectuals to regard the
Russian peasant as a "natural socialist."

In the half-century after the Emancipation Russia's agrarian situation went from bad to worse. This was due primarily to rural overpopulation, the outcome of Russia's remarkable population growth
during the nineteenth century, whose effects were compounded by

legal obstacles and meager opportunity for leaving the land. Furthermore, serfdom before 1861 and the commune system afterward discouraged modernization in farming methods, and Russian crop yields
remained among the world's lowest. Only the newly developed
capitalistic agriculture of the Black Sea coastal region was an exception, and it was this area that produced most of Russia's increasing grain exports of the nineteenth century. Elsewhere in the
country successful peasants chipped away at their landlords' holdings
by purchase, as the nobility sold land to supplement their declining
incomes. Private estates—which accounted for about half of European Russia before 1861, about 25 per cent after the Emancipation
—were reduced to some 10 or 15 per cent of the total land area on
the eve of World War I. But population increase and the continued
subdivision of their plots kept the peasants' land hunger alive and
still tempted them to solve their problems by revolutionary seizure
of the nobles' remaining lands.

The increase in Russia's population all through the nineteenth
century confutes some of the standard rules of demography. At the
death of Peter the Great in 1725 Russia had an estimated population
of 13 million. This approximated the contemporary population of
the German states and was considerably less than the more highly
developed and productive 20 million of France, at that time the leading European power. Surprisingly enough, when the population of
Russia began its rapid increase—presumably due to a decline in the
death rate—it occurred without much industrial, technological, or
medical progress and actually under conditions of near slavery.

By the end of the eighteenth century the population of Russia
(as defined by the boundaries of 1725) had more than doubled to
nearly 30 million, to whom were added perhaps seven or eight million
inhabitants of the Polish and Turkish lands conquered by Catherine
the Great. The Russian Empire was now the most populous state in
Europe. Rapid population growth continued in Russia in the nineteenth century, and the total nearly doubled again between 1800
and the Emancipation of 1861. The first Russian census, in 1897,
reported 125 million. This trend severely aggravated the pressure of
rural overpopulation and land hunger, even though the government
was finally permitting free migration to Siberia and industrialization
was beginning to offer an escape from the land into the cities.

The population of the Russian Empire had reached perhaps 170
million at the time of the Revolution, but this was substantially
reduced by the postwar independence of Poland, Finland, and the
Baltic states, as well as by the mortality of war, civil strife, and

famine. The population of the USSR according to the first Soviet census in 1926 was 147 million, approximately 120 million of whom still lived in rural areas. From this time on, the rural population of the Soviet Union has remained relatively stable, with the higher natural increase of the villages balanced by migration into the cities for employment in the rapidly growing Soviet industrial establishment. A second Soviet census was taken in 1937, but the disappointing results were suppressed and the census takers purged. A new census in 1939 reported a total of 170 million, of whom 55 million lived in the cities.

In recent decades Soviet Russia's rate of population increase has begun to drop off in the manner of most countries which have become substantially urbanized, but it was the impact of World War II that truly retarded Soviet population growth. Soviet military losses (combatants killed or prisoners starved) were probably around 10 million, with additional millions of civilian deaths directly or indirectly attributable to the war. Even more severe was the drop in the birth rate during the war years. As a result of all these factors, the Soviet Union in 1959, though territorially larger, had only 209 million people, just 20 million more than the population of 1939. The population of the United States, by contrast, increased by about 40 million in the same period.

Calculations of population should bear in mind that the Soviet population is still, on the whole, more backward and more rural than that of Western Europe and North America. Rural overpopulation and underproduction are still a drag on the Soviet economic system. At the present time the Soviet economy is only a partial fulfillment of the process of modernization and industrialization begun in the 1880s and 1890s.

The onset of industrialization toward the end of the nineteenth century marked the true beginning of the westernization of Russian society. Its consequences were immediately revolutionary. In a later chapter we will examine this period of transformation and its relation to the Russian Revolution.

Russian Culture: Orthodoxy vs. Westernization

Cultural and intellectual life in Russia has always had an unnatural relation to the rest of society. Because of the influence of more highly civilized neighbors, Russian culture has never had an opportunity to grow naturally and independently. It has often developed beyond what the country might sustain on its own, but it has sometimes stagnated when the foreign sources were shut off. In tsarist and Soviet times alike Russian thinking has been plagued by conflict between native and foreign values, and by a national inferiority complex.

Civilized cultural activity began in Russia with the Christianization of the country and the establishment of Greek Orthodoxy as the state religion in Kievan times. With the Church and its largely Greek clergy came the first systematic education and the first use of writing among the Russians, using the Church Slavonic dialect of the Balkans which was written in the Cyrillic alphabet devised by St. Cyril and Methodius to translate the Holy Scriptures into the Slavic tongue. Church Slavonic, differing from spoken Russian rather less than Latin differs from Italian, remained the language of the Church and of most written communication in Russia until the seventeenth century.

Apart from folklore and chronicles, Kievan culture was strictly ecclesiastical, and even within that realm achievements of a philosophical nature were conspicuously few. The tradition of the Russian Orthodox Church is highly ritualistic and mystical, with a pronounced aversion to what many Russians have regarded as the cold excesses of rationalism and legalism in the Western Churches, both Catholic and Protestant. On the other hand, the Kievan Church, though it barred statuary and instrumental music, developed a vigorous tradition in the visual arts of ikon painting and religious architecture which persisted until modern times.

Kiev was closely dependent on Byzantium not only for cultural inspiration but for much of its ecclesiastical personnel as well, and when nomadic invasions culminating in the Mongol conquest severed Russia's ties with the south, cultural development ceased. As in Western Europe in the Dark Ages, the Church did scarcely more than preserve the culture of the past, while the masses lived on in unlettered ignorance. Politically and economically, however, the Orthodox Church figured prominently during the Mongol period and in connection with the rise of Muscovy. Monasteries took a leading part in colonizing and developing new lands in the northeastern quadrant of European Russia, and in the early modern period perhaps a fourth of the country's arable area was owned by the Church.

In the thirteenth and fourteenth centuries, after the Mongol conquest and the expansion of Lithuania, the Russian Orthodox Church, like the nation as a whole, was split. Kiev, which had its own Metropolitan (archbishop), fell under Lithuanian and later Polish rule. This exposed it to Western influence, and it became in time a relatively sophisticated cultural center. Toward the end of the sixteenth century the Poles effected a union of some of the Orthodox

Ukrainians under their jurisdiction with the Church of Rome. This was the origin of the so-called Uniate Church, or Catholic Church of the Eastern Rite, acknowledging the supremacy of the Pope but retaining the liturgy and rules of the Orthodox Church, including the Church Slavonic language in worship and the marriage of parish priests. Much of the western part of the Ukraine (Galicia) became Uniate and remained so until the Soviet Union finally annexed the area during World War II and forcibly reunited the Uniates with the Orthodox Church.

The rest of the medieval Russian Church, in the lands under Mongol rule, had its center in Moscow after 1326. Under the Metropolitan of Moscow, the Church was the one united and national organization in what later became Muscovite Russia and provided a focus for the growth of Russian national consciousness. On the other hand, cut off even from Kiev—let alone Byzantium—the Muscovite Church exercised no intellectual leadership or cultural innovation.

The association of Russia's religious center with Moscow was an important factor in the successful aspiration of the Muscovite princes to lead the nascent Russian national state. Further, the Church fed the imperial ambitions of the Muscovite tsars with the theory of the Third Rome and messianic ideas of Russia's Christian mission. Thanks to the Turkish conquest of Byzantium and the Balkans, Muscovite Russia was indeed the only independent Greek Orthodox state from the fifteenth century to the nineteenth, and the notion of a national mission to perpetuate the one true faith was a naturally persisting one.

Church and state cooperated closely in Muscovy. The Church commanded of its faithful an absolute submission to the state, and the state persecuted every evidence of religious dissent or criticism as treason. Rationalistic heresies which paralleled some of the religious currents of the Western Renaissance and Reformation were rooted out. Jews were barred from the country altogether until the eighteenth century acquisition of Polish and Turkish territories with large Jewish minorities.

In the sixteenth and seventeenth centuries the Orthodox Church was closely tied to the government personally as well as institutionally. Paralleling the practice of medieval and early modern Europe, the tsars drew many of their top officials from the Church. The status of the Church itself was enhanced in 1589 when the Metropolitan of Moscow was raised to the rank of Patriarch, giving Moscow theoretical equality with Constantinople and the other traditional patriarchates of the Orthodox Church. The Patriarchs of Moscow were key national leaders during the Time of Troubles. Tsar Michael, elected in 1613, was the son of Patriarch Filaret, who was the real ruler of the country while he lived.

In 1654 Russia acquired the Eastern Ukraine together with the city of Kiev. Contact with Kiev dramatized certain points of scriptural and ritualistic deviation which had occurred within the Muscovite Church, and prompted Patriarch Nikon to order the appropriate corrections to bring Russian practice into line with the standard of Constantinople. This involved such minor innovations as crossing oneself with three fingers instead of two. Nikon overreached himself in his political ambitions and was deposed by Tsar Alexei, but the government nonetheless adhered to Nikon's reforms. The main significance of these liturgical changes is the astounding resistance which they encountered among the Russian populace. Opponents of the reform broke with the Church altogether, despite vicious governmental persecution. In this schism of the 1650s and 1660s lay the origin of the Old Believers and of the proliferation of anarchistic sects to which this opposition group gave rise. Until the Revolution perhaps 20 per cent of the Russian population followed these sects in protest against all central authority, secular or religious, that contaminated itself with reform and change.

Nikon's reform of the Church was pale in comparison to the impact of Peter the Great and the westernization which he and his successors espoused. By inclination a rowdy blasphemer and by policy a secularizer, Peter destroyed the political influence of the Church. He abolished the office of Patriarch and reduced the Church to the official status of a government department under a lay chief, the Procurator of the Holy Synod. His successors were Machiavellians who kept the Church as an instrument of rule over the masses, while they personally patronized the rationalism of the Enlightenment. Catherine the Great secularized most of the lands of the Church and put the entire clergy in the status of lowly civil servants. The typical parish priest was the impoverished and illiterate but hereditary tenant of his position.

Imperial endorsement of the intellectual position of the Church became much firmer after the shocks of the French Revolution and the Napoleonic Wars. Special efforts were made to force Orthodoxy on minorities such as Roman Catholics and Jews. However, the Church as an institution never recovered its earlier political, economic, or cultural stature. It was nearly dead already when it was assaulted by the revolutionary legislation of the Bolsheviks, and

Russia finally became an entirely secular state both in law and in policy.

The growth of the empire gave Russia a diversity of religions as well as nationalities, though with the Church-state tie of tsarism religious variety was impossible for the regime to tolerate with equanimity. The Orthodox Church was always privileged and preferred, though the minority faiths generally held their own against persecution. This accounts for the present religious situation which we have already described, with Lutheranism and Catholicism persisting in the Baltic states and Islam in Central Asia and parts of the Caucasus, in addition to the Jewish and sectarian minorities throughout Great Russia and the Ukraine.

The reign of Peter was the great turning point not only in Russia's religious and political life but above all in its cultural and intellectual life. The arrested ecclesiastical culture of Muscovite Russia, defended by the state against corrupting outside influences, now became the object of a systematic attack by the government itself. Previous Russian contact with the West was largely confined to such matters as trade, architecture, and the military arts. Peter set his aim as the deliberate incorporation of Western civilization into Russia and of Russia into Western civilization. Specifically, the Western civilization which he aimed to import meant Western technology (from glass manufacturing to shipbuilding), Western education (mainly for its military and technical benefit), and Western manners for the nobility (ranging from tableware and handkerchiefs to the admission of women into formal social life). Underlying all this, of course, was Peter's desire to enter Western civilization as a diplomatic and military participant.

Peter's actual cultural accomplishments fell far short of his aspirations. Western culture was absorbed only in the most crudely superficial manner, only by the upper class, and only through methods of oriental despotism. For example, Peter would command the sons of the nobility to be educated and enforce this by banning their marriage until they had completed their schooling. Russia still had no institutions of higher learning apart from the theological seminaries and the German-speaking University of Dorpat which Peter acquired in his conquest of the Baltic coast from Sweden. Peter did establish an Academy of Sciences—forerunner of the present Soviet institution —but it had to be staffed by foreigners, and its Russian students were fewer in number than its foreign scholars.

Many of Peter's other reforms were just as superficial and limited. He adopted the Western calendar instead of reckoning the years from the creation of the world, but it was the Julian calendar, which had already been supplanted in the Catholic world by the more accurate Gregorian calendar. Peter also changed the written script from the Gothic-looking Cyrillic of the Church Slavonic to a new "civil type" on cleaner Latin lines—but it was still Cyrillic, when he could have gone over to the Roman alphabet altogether.

The importance of Peter's innovations in culture lay in what they symbolized or implied rather than in what they actually accomplished. For a century thereafter the government was the deliberate agent of westernization: the sponsor of Western education in Russia (the University of Moscow was founded 1755) or of education for Russians in the West, the patron of Western styles in theater and literature and of Western philosophy in the fashion of the Enlightenment. This work was aided by the Russian annexation of the Baltic provinces of Estonia and Latvia, which were dominated by German landowners descended from the Teutonic Knights of the Middle Ages. These Baltic Barons were a major source of intellectual and administrative talent for the Russian government throughout the eighteenth and into the nineteenth century. They were particularly proficient in running the secret police, which has always operated, then as now, with remarkably un-Russian efficiency. Meanwhile, one native Russian won for his country a claim to real international respect in the Age of the Enlightenment: Mikhail Lomonosov, a fisherman's son from the Arctic coast, who shone forth as poet, historian, and linguistic scientist, and as one of the principal founders of the modern science of chemistry.

The experience which Peter initiated for Russia is that known to social science as acculturation—changes in a society's culture and way of life through contact with a stronger foreign culture. Russia was actually the first major country to feel the full impact of the profound world-wide process of acculturation known as westernization. Russia's acculturation began with an interest in technical and practical matters and was warmly endorsed by the government. But opening the lines of communication to the West meant the intrusion of Western ideas and values as well, and these sooner or later undermined the whole established order of Russian belief and practice—political, religious, social, and economic. Acculturation was uneven and inconsistent; it served to underscore the residual backwardness of the country; it sharpened the social division of the classes into a gaping cultural cleavage between the westernized nobility and the "dark people"; and it made traditional rights seem indefensible wrongs. The educated classes, as they often do when similarly alienated from their heritage, went to the two extremes of revolutionary repudiation of their own society or messianic reaffirmation of it. Communism, in Russia and in Asia as well, might be regarded as a strange synthesis of these two contradictory responses to westernization, a sort of anti-Western westernizing.

In the nineteenth century Russian culture blossomed phenomenally under the most inauspicious conditions. Alien in its own country and confined to the literate few, it was still helped along by state sponsorship of an increasing number of schools and universities. Cultural activity lost governmental favor after the French Revolution and the Napoleonic Wars and thereafter had to struggle most of the time against an obscurantist if inefficient censorship. Nevertheless, Russian intellectual life in the last three quarters of the nineteenth century reached its creative zenith and made a major contribution to the international civilization of the West in a variety of fields. Russian literature—Pushkin's poetry, the novels of Gogol, Turgenev, Tolstoy, and Dostoevsky, the drama of Chekhov—was unparalleled anywhere in the world. No energetic tradition developed in the visual arts, but nineteenth-century Russian music contributed many major works to the classical repertoire. Russians stood in the forefront of scientific work, with a distinctive bent toward mathematics and theory, such as Mendeleyev's Periodic Law in chemistry. The field most hobbled by political control was that of social and political thought, but even here Russia developed vigorous if often naive philosophies and controversies.

The social vehicle of all this intellectual ferment in nineteenth-century Russia was a particular class—if it may be called that—the intelligentsia. "Intelligentsia" is actually a Russian word, designating in the nineteenth century all those people who produced ideas and also the large group of the educated who provided the audience for ideas.*

The intelligentsia was originally drawn from the nobility and landed gentry, though after the middle of the nineteenth century individuals from every other social order (the so-called *raznochintsy* or "men of various ranks") achieved membership in it. The intelligentsia was cut off from power and practical pursuits. Its style of thought quickly became set in a mold that was profoundly critical and highly theoretical, the antithesis of Anglo-American pragmatism. As avid borrowers of Western thought—from Hegel and the German

* In Soviet usage the "intelligentsia" includes all pen-pushers and white-collar workers, but the cultural distinctiveness of this class probably still justifies the term.

idealists through the French utopian socialists to Karl Marx and the scientific materialism of the later nineteenth century—the Russian intelligentsia adopted European philosophies more intensely and dogmatically than their Western originators ever did. Marx himself said that the young Russian aristocrats were "always running after the most extreme that the West can offer." He added prophetically, "This does not prevent the same Russians from becoming scoundrels once they enter the service of the government."

By the 1840s two distinct currents of opinion took shape among the intelligentsia. These responses to the challenge of Western civilization resembled the schizophrenic reactions which have distinguished many cultures subjected to acculturation. The so-called Westerners advocated outright assimilation to the West. They saw the reign of Peter the Great as the point when Russia had been led out of darkness, and favored an effort to follow the West European development of freedom, rationalism, science, and industry, with the hope that Russia could even overtake and surpass the West. The other group, known as the Slavophiles, were messianic nativists —Westernized intellectuals to be sure—who looked romantically back to pre-Petrine traditions and found Russia's strength in the peasant, his commune, and the mystical virtue of the Russian Orthodox Church. Neither Westerners nor Slavophiles were held in high favor by the government, which under Nicholas I espoused its own creed of "orthodoxy, autocracy, nationality."

The Westerners and the tradition of thought they initiated proved to be the seedbed of Russian revolutionary thought and action and the intellectual foundation of the Soviet regime. The Westerners for the most part believed in reason and science, perhaps so intensely that they made a religion out of science, as Communism still does. The Westerners were believers in progress, material, educational, and institutional. Influenced by their greatest spokesman, Alexander Herzen, they aspired less to the current society of the West and more to the future vision of Western critics—namely, socialism. Mikhail Bakunin added to this his philosophy of anarchism and a code of revolutionary conspiracy. Nikolai Chernyshevsky expounded the possibility of economic progress through cooperative socialism in a nation of peasants.

Out of all these ideas there crystallized by the 1870s a distinctive revolutionary movement with a distinctive Russian revolutionary philosophy. The philosophy was Populism, a belief in the establishment of socialism based on the communal life of the peasants. The movement had two currents, one of agitation among the masses, the other of terroristic conspiracy. Populism and its various manifestations of revolutionary action drew the battle lines between government and nation and set the stage for the impending upheaval of revolution.

Meanwhile, Slavophile nativism was absorbed by pro-government spokesmen of nationalism in the second half of the nineteenth century to produce the reactionary, aggressive doctrine of Pan-Slavism exemplified by Dostoevsky. "Our great Russia," he wrote, "at the head of the united Slavs, will utter to the world her new . . . and as yet unheard word . . . for the good and genuine unification of mankind as a whole in a new, brotherly, universal union whose inception is derived from the Slavic genius, preeminently from the spirit of the great Russian people who have suffered so long. . . ." *

One final development in Russia's prerevolutionary intellectual history should be noted: the remarkable development of modernism beginning in the 1890s in many fields of Russian thought and culture. From music (Stravinsky), painting (Kandinsky), and literature (the symbolists) to philosophy and social thought Russians broke down conventional forms and standards. The Revolution was really accomplished by representatives of the older rationalist-materialist school which the most creative intellects were leaving behind, but the cultural innovators who remained in Russia generally sympathized with the Soviet regime. Ironically, the whole stream of modernism in Russia was shut off almost with one blow by Stalin in the early 1930s, when the more traditional rationalist, representational, and disciplinarian standards of thought and life were made a binding orthodoxy for the Soviet state.

The Russian Past and the Soviet State

Russia is still Russia. Such a fact is scarcely worth mentioning with respect to most countries, but in the case of Russia—with its recent experience of cataclysmic revolution, domination by a new faith, and drastic overhaul of its institutions—the underlying continuities are easy to overlook. It is therefore important to sum up the various ways in which elements of the Russian past have come through all the changes of the present century and how these elements express themselves directly or indirectly in the present character of the Soviet state.

Soviet Russia today is the same country as the empire of the tsars. It occupies the same geography; comprises the same people; speaks the same dominant language and the same diverse minority tongues;

* Fyodor Dostoevsky, *Diary of a Writer*, II, 780.

exhibits the same general culture in the anthropological sense, with little more disruption than other agricultural civilizations have experienced in the course of industrialization. Soviet Russa still faces the same kind of international temptations and dangers and navigates in its international environment with a not too different combination of caution, deviousness, and force. Internally the Soviet state must still deal with a society in which anything that is going to be done effectively must be done by the state and under compulsion. Finally, the truly great changes accomplished by the Soviet state—its industrialization and its modernization of a peasant society—represent a direct continuation of the efforts of every tsar from Peter the Great to Nicholas II, pursued, moreover, by the same methods of compulsion and with the same distrust of individual purpose or initiative.

More concretely, an analysis of Soviet political organization and methods points directly back to prerevolutionary native experience and not to any foreign ideology. The realities of the Soviet government contradict Marxist theory at every point, but they coincide closely with the essential features of tsarism: autocratic power at the top, rule through a bureaucracy, reliance on the secret police and Siberia to rule out opposition, complete centralization of authority with no real local autonomy, resort to the state in the last instance to settle every sort of question. In both tsarism and Soviet Communism political power subordinates all other aspects of society to itself, denies any essential right of opposition or independence, and to a greater or lesser degree distrusts and curbs any sort of nongovernmental organization or initiative. The Russian background, in short, contained substantial elements of totalitarianism which the Revolution failed to offset.

Corresponding to the traditional power of the state was the traditional weakness of organized nongovernmental activity in Russia. The higher orders of society—Church, merchants, and (after the sixteenth century) nobility—were submissive. The masses were anarchic but powerless, and periodic outbursts of crowd violence did nothing to qualify the autocratic structure of the state. To be sure, nonpolitical society grew stronger with the development of modern industry, business organizations, and professions in the late nineteenth century. But after the Revolution all these modern institutions were absorbed into the totalitarian state. Communism, in the broadest perspective, imprisons modernity within the shackles of the Russian autocratic tradition.

Finally, we must note the impact of tsarism on its own opponents.

Reformers in every society mirror, to a degree, the established order; in Russia it was natural that successful reformers could only be autocratic aspirants to total power. A recurring image in Russian political thought is the "tsar-revolutionary," the leader with the will to overturn society and the autocratic power to make this will a reality. Such attitudes were deeply imbedded in the Russian revolutionary tradition, and they made the Soviet restoration of autocracy seem almost natural.

There are, of course, many novel features in Soviet rule and thought, but these stem more from the pre-Marxist Russian revolutionary movement than from Marxism itself. Among the enduring political attitudes generated by the earlier movement were the idea of the conspiratorial party, the creed of dogmatic materialism and antireligious fervor, the rejection of all private money-making activity, and a highly ambivalent reaction to the West as both model and corrupter. To put it dialectically, Soviet Russia is the synthesis of the tsarist thesis and the revolutionary antithesis, embellished with the language of a borrowed Western creed.

One final way in which the tsarist past can be held accountable for the Soviet present is the fact that the old order led to a total revolution. A great revolution, as we shall note in the next chapter, has distinctive characteristics as a particular kind of historical process, although the place and time of its occurrence depend on local circumstances and are not foreordained. The possibility of a major social revolution in twentieth-century Russia must be explained in terms of social circumstances and institutional weaknesses in the prerevolutionary order.

Naturally, it is impossible to explain the Soviet picture wholly in terms of the prerevolutionary background, any more than the present physiognomy of any other nation is wholly derived from its historical experience. The particular doctrine which prevailed in the Revolution was new and had its impact. Much that happened in the course of the Revolution and later on in Soviet history was a matter of political accident or of personalities. Finally, and most important, Soviet Russia was born into an international environment that was undergoing political and technological changes of revolutionary scope. Perhaps more than meets the eye, the course of Soviet development has been a response (though not the only possible one) to the common international challenges of war, totalitarian politics, and the world-wide spread of the Industrial Revolution. Soviet Russia is no longer the old Russia, but only in the measure that any country in the world today can no longer be its old historical self.

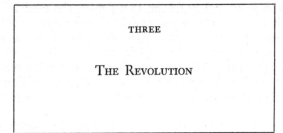

THREE

THE REVOLUTION

Great revolutions are in a class by themselves as rare but kindred historical events. Their effects are vast and profound. It is no surprise that the Russian Revolution should have proved to be not only the great turning point in the history of Russia but an event of far-reaching significance for the history of the entire world. The Russian Revolution was among the first and most volcanic responses to the modern world's vast and unique transformation through westernization. As such, the Russian upheaval is a model that no one else can ignore. More compellingly, the Russian Revolution, as revolution *per se* and as the expression of a mighty empire, was the father of a powerful new politico-religious movement that offered its fiery salvation to the West and non-West alike. Barring atomic war, the Russian Revolution will certainly go down in history as the greatest event of modern times.

The Nature of Revolution

The Russian Revolution was, as we have suggested, one of a numerically small but distinctive and overwhelmingly important class of historical events—the great social revolutions. The class includes, of course, the great French Revolution, the English Puritan Revolution of the seventeenth century, the Chinese Revolution that commenced in 1911 and is still going on, and similar upheavals in lesser countries, such as the Mexican Revolution of the 1910s and 1920s. Perhaps the experience of Germany from 1918 to 1945 might be regarded as a somewhat deviant case in the same general group.

What all of these instances of revolution have in common is the complete breakdown of the old institutions of governmental authority and social control, followed by a distinctive process of violent and painful events lasting some 10 to 20 years before adequate authority and order are restored. The great revolutions are quite different from the simpler types of "revolution"—the coup d'état, where authority changes hands violently without greatly altering the nature of governmental authority, and the national revolution, where a region or a colony fights to detach itself from the authority of an outside political center without necessarily altering the internal institutions of the area.

The great social revolutions were all brewed in similar historical situations of social change balked by political rigidity. They generally involved tradition-bound monarchies which could not accommodate themselves to rising forces of commercialism or industrialism and tried blindly but ineffectually to uphold the old order of authority, privilege, and belief. The great revolutions were not the result of misery, which has been endemic in mankind's experience, but of progress—progress that was cramped—with the rise of groups whose political power did not match their social and economic importance.

The great revolution typically began not by plot but by accident, when some crisis such as a financial impasse or a military defeat shook the authority of the monarchy and enabled the populace to cast off its traditional obedience. The English Revolution and the French Revolution originated in the monarchy's need for money and the convocation of representatives (Parliament and Estates-General) who then defied the king. The Russian Revolution of 1917 and the German Revolution of 1918 were born out of the adverse fortunes of war. The first stage of most revolutions was relatively easy and relatively moderate.

The trouble besetting the moderate revolutionary regimes, particularly the Provisional Government set up after the February Revolution in Russia, was the witches' cauldron of conflicting social forces and long pent-up grievances which the weakening of the old authority uncovered. Mass readiness to obey was not enjoyed by the moderate revolutionaries. Quite the contrary: classes, parties, and sects began to struggle on behalf of their particular views with no readiness to submit or compromise. Public order degenerated until some group or party—revolutionary or counterrevolutionary—appeared with the requisite discipline, organization, and force to impose its own minority will as a dictatorship over all the other contending minorities in the nation. Thus did the revolutionary nation, in most cases, enter the phase of extremist dictatorship: England under Cromwell and his Independents (Congregationalists) in 1648; France under the Jacobins in 1792; Russia under the Bolsheviks in the October Revolution of 1917; Germany under Adolf Hitler and the Nazis in 1933.

The extremist dictatorship was a time of utopian and puritanical experiment, rammed down the nation's throat by force and fanaticism. The particular ideals and programs of the several revolutions varied widely, from the religious moralism of the English Revolution and the bourgeois rationalism and nationalism of the French, to the race myth of the Nazis, but the methods and spirit of revolutionary dictatorship were essentially the same. All the extremist regimes embraced some all-encompassing doctrine with the fervor of a new religious faith, whether the doctrine was literally a religion as in the English Revolution, or secular dogmas such as the Jacobins, Communists, and Nazis professed.

The extreme phase of revolution was always, by its very nature, relatively brief. It generally proved impossible for the revolutionaries to sustain their utopian drive against the majority of the nation, and either the revolutionaries had to make practical compromises or they were overthrown. Cromwell had to tone down his Puritanism in the 1650s, and his Commonwealth was overthrown altogether after his death in the Restoration of 1660. The Jacobins in France were overthrown in the Thermidorean Reaction of 1794 (so called from the coup d'état of July 27, or 9 Thermidor, according to the revolutionary calendar). The Bolsheviks in Russia made their own adjustment in 1921 just in time to hold power by jettisoning the heart of their revolutionary program. Hitler did somewhat the same in 1934.

Along with this readjustment after the extremist phase, the great revolutions all exhibited a continuing concentration of dictatorial authority. This was pursued by the extremist dictator as he readjusted his program (Cromwell in England and Hitler in Germany) or by some quasi-revolutionary successor after the readjustment had occurred (Napoleon Bonaparte in France and Joseph Stalin in Russia).

Last of all, the postrevolutionary dictatorships usually ran afoul of enemies, foreign or domestic, and were overthrown. Some form of "restoration" of the old regime followed—or rather, a return to the initial setup of the moderate revolution. This was the outcome when domestic discord and a military coup brought King Charles II to England in 1660, sharing his power with Parliament. The French Restoration of 1815, following the military defeat of Napoleon, was a return to the semiconstitutional monarchy of 1789. Hitler's defeat in 1945 paved the way for a new and healthier version of the moderate Weimar Republic in present-day West Germany. Only in Soviet Russia and Communist China has there been no overt restoration.

While events in Russia in the last half-century have clearly had much in common with the recurring pattern of the great revolutions, there are other factors to consider which help explain some of the more distinctive features of the Russian Revolution. The Russian

Revolution occurred amid circumstances of a unique transformation in the history of civilization—that is, the familiar changes of the Industrial Revolution, together with the process of westernization. In the past century every civilization outside the old European-North American zone of Western culture has come under the impact of Western political, cultural, and economic influence, including rapid though uneven commercialization and industrialization. Referring back to the scheme of great revolutions as the product of social progress and political cramp, we can observe that the basic cause of the Russian and other non-European revolutions of this century was the progress of industrialization and westernization that could not be politically accommodated by old monarchical or colonial regimes. Russia is the prototype and model for the revolution-in-the-course-of-westernizing, entirely apart from any influence of the Marxist-Leninist revolutionary ideology which the Russians adopted.

At the same time, Russia in revolution was sufficiently Western and modern to partake of another international phenomenon—totalitarianism. Totalitarianism may be summed up as dictatorial rule using all the most modern means of control—organization, communications, and weapons—and recognizing no limits to its power. It is the characteristic twentieth-century form of the extremist revolutionary or postrevolutionary dictatorship. The very possibility of totalitarianism rests on modern Western developments—technology on the one hand, and on the other, the tendency to marshal most aspects of life into large organizations. The twentieth-century revolution often culminates in a dictatorship prepared to push the totalitarian strains in modern life to their logical conclusion.

Finally, we should note how the revolutions of Communism and nationalism represent a reaction against the dominance of the West. The reaction is ambivalent, as we noted in the case of the nineteenth-century Russian intelligentsia. Educated non-Western leaders want to copy the West, but they resent its superiority, and if they can find some Western doctrine of criticism as a standard for outdoing the West itself, they will do so eagerly. This is fundamentally why Marxism took hold so firmly in Russia and is so popular throughout the underdeveloped world, where the proletarian revolution is largely irrelevant. In these regions Marxism has become a vehicle for anti-Western westernizing. We will see in the history of political dissension in Soviet Russia during the first 15 years after the Revolution how the Marxist faith was changed around to fit this challenge of the westernizing revolution.

The Background of Revolution in Russia

The Russian Revolution was the outcome of two centuries of Russian history, the dramatic resolution of the profound clash between monarchical tradition and the thought and industry taken from the West. The Revolution was a thoroughly Russian event, though it followed a universal pattern. Russia even today cannot be fully understood without recognizing the forces that brought the Revolution about.

More clearly than in any other country, the Revolution in Russia was the result of sweeping social change under the old government. Peter the Great and his successors, by inviting the cultural westernization of the Russian upper class, began the intellectual undermining of the foundations of traditional authority. Events from the time of the French Revolution to the Decembrist conspiracy caused the Russian monarchy to turn away from the Western model, but it was too late to curb the critical ferment among the newly formed intelligentsia. A far longer history of conscious revolutionary thought, agitation, and organization preceded the Russian Revolution than any other. This process was drawn out so long because the intellectual inspiration from the West was far ahead of what the mass of Russian society was at first ready to accept.

The Russian revolutionary movement consisted of a series of Western-inspired efforts to achieve an eighteenth-century utopia in a land of Dark Age despotism. The revolutionary intellectuals, starting with the Decembrists, were educated, frustrated, and morally committed; they embraced scientific rationalism and drew away from the Church; they subscribed to an anticommercial socialism with the peasant as its focus and strove to implement this ideal by every revolutionary means. Their first herald was Alexander Radishchev (1749-1802), exiled by Catherine the Great for his critique of serfdom and absolutism. The radical Decembrists of the Southern Society, headed by Colonel Paul Pestel, added the program of a dictatorial revolutionary republic. The great Russian synthesis of philosophical materialism, revolution, socialism, and the peasant tradition was the work of Alexander Herzen (1812-1870), who quit the country after suffering provincial exile and spent the rest of his life in England and France calling for the ultimate upheaval in Russia.

Russian revolutionary thought and action after Herzen assumed various schismatic forms. Mikhail Bakunin (1814-1876) espoused the philosophy of immediate anarchism—agitation for a mass uprising in the Pugachov style that would destroy government, Church, and property alike and liberate society into a "federation of self-governing communes." Bakunin's direct influence was felt more in the Mediterranean countries than in Russia, but his tactics of conspiratorial organization were emulated by a series of Russian groups in the 1860s and 1870s. These were the so-called Russian Jacobins, exemplified by the mad plotter Sergei Nechaev and by the "People's Will" organization that assassinated Alexander II.

The Russian intellectuals of the 1860s were distinguished by the creed of nihilism—a faith in scientific materialism, criticism of all accepted institutions and values, and the belief in a rationally reconstructed society of free, equal, and selfless citizens. The most important exponent of this outlook was Nikolai Chernyshevsky (1828-1889), whose essays and utopian novel *What Is To Be Done?*, revolving around the potentiality for enlightened individual leadership, had a powerful influence on succeeding generations of revolutionaries. Lenin acknowledged his intellectual debt to Chernyshevsky, and it was in reality a greater one than he owed to Marx.

The late 1860s and 1870s saw the greatest surge of revolutionary activity of the entire nineteenth century. It was tactically more gradualist than the Bakunists and centered on the loose body of doctrine known as Populism. Populism was a program for intellectuals, motivated by enlightened moral responsibility, to appeal to the masses through various tactics of education and agitation. It was a distinctively Russian program to achieve socialism by avoiding capitalism of the Western sort and basing the revolution on the peasants. But the masses were not ready in the 1870s, and Populism proved a failure.

The assassination of Alexander II in 1881 signaled a period of severe political repression under the reactionary police rule of his son Alexander III. Only in the mid-1890s, following the accession of Nicholas II, did revolutionary activity inside Russia significantly revive. Now, however, the revolutionaries were much more successful in appealing to the masses. The reason for this was simply the progress of westernization and the new mass impact of modern industry and commercialized agriculture.

While Russian manufacturing had grown gradually during the nineteenth century, true industrialization with the modern factory system and the large-scale use of modern technology did not commence until the 1880s. Two forces were instrumental in the onset of industrialization at that time: foreign capital and the tsarist government itself. While politically and socially unyielding, the government of Tsar Alexander III was not averse to promoting modern business

enterprise by the mercantilist methods and for the mercantilist purposes which Peter the Great had exemplified in his own turn to the
West—to enhance the power of the Russian state. The tsars, like
the Soviet regime, were compelled to borrow the achievements of the
West, and then had to try to blunt the political implications of such
borrowing. Specifically, Alexander III adopted the gold standard,
built railroads, set up protective tariffs and subsidies, and kept trade
unions illegal. Foreign capital, especially British, French, and Belgian,
poured in to exploit Russia's mineral resources and to lay the iron-
and-steel foundations of a modern heavy industry. By 1913 Russia
had the world's fifth-largest industrial plant (after the United States,
Germany, Britain, and France). About half of this plant was owned
by foreign interests.

Russian industrialization was rapid but uneven and unsettling.
Certain regions—the Donets Basin with its coal and steel, the Moscow province with its textile industry, St. Petersburg and its environs
with the manufacture of machinery and railroad rolling stock, the
Baku oil area, and the Ural mining area—became as urban, industrial,
and advanced as any in the world. The size of the average factory in
Russia was larger than in any country in Europe. But most of Russia
remained rural and backward. The availability of surplus labor from
the villages kept urban wages and conditions poor. The rate of illiteracy, though falling, was still over 50 per cent of the adult population on the eve of the Revolution.

Industrialization created in Russia a modern working class and a
modern middle class, both of which had been lacking before. Both
groups—the business and professional men as well as the workers in
the factory barracks, were politically ignored and frustrated by the
monarchy. By the 1890s both groups began to heed the talk of revolutionaries. Likewise the peasants, seeing opportunity in the cities,
hungry for land and aware of an increasingly unequal distribution of
wealth in the countryside, began to lend an ear to the plans and
promises of the revolutionaries. By the early 1900s almost everyone
in Russia was ready for revolution of one sort or another.

With growing popular support for their activities, the reviving
Russian revolutionary organizations of the 1890s divided into three
competing political parties, based on three different class followings,
though most of the leaders of all three groups came from the intelligentsia. A liberal movement, taking as its model the constitutional
monarchy of Great Britain or the French Republic, attracted much
of the professional class and some of the more open-minded gentry.
Liberals organized the Constitutional Democratic Party (Kadets,

from the Russian initials K and D) in 1905. The allegiance of most peasants went to the revived Populist movement, the Socialist Revolutionary Party (SR's), set up in 1900. Some of the industrial workers followed the SR's as well, though more lined up behind a new movement on the Russian scene, the Marxists, who founded the Russian Social Democratic Workers' Party in 1898. Out of this group, of course, came the leadership and the ideology of the Soviet dictatorship and the international Communist movement.

Marxism

Marxism, with certain emendations and interpretations, was and is the official philosophy of the party whose seizure of power in 1917 created Russia's extremist revolutionary dictatorship and the governmental structure prevailing to this day. The thought and actions of the Communists throughout the history of the Soviet regime have been couched in Marxist terms, and though the philosophy cannot account for much of what the Communists have done, it must be understood in its essentials in order to comprehend the Communist mind and the peculiar relation of theory and practice in the Communist system.

There are at first sight some striking incongruities in the Communist attachment to Marxist doctrine. Russia was not the highly industrialized sort of country where, according to the central argument of Marxism, the proletarian revolution against capitalism would first take place. The Communists nevertheless claim to represent such a revolution, but the objective observer should be careful not to assume the validity of Marxist terms in describing events in Russia. Communism dogmatically asserts the vital importance of correct Marxist belief, though the theory itself suggests that beliefs depend on and reflect material realities. Communist practice in Russia and elsewhere seems to contravene the Marxist ideals of moneyless equality and withering of governmental authority, though verbally these ideals are still held up as future goals. Marxism's appeal has been felt most strongly not in the fully industrial countries or among the members of a mature working class, but in countries in the early stages of industrialization, and among the alienated students and intellectuals of such regions more than among the local proletarians. The political career of Marxism has not corresponded to the movement's own theory of history, and this is one reason that the doctrine can be kept intact only within the confines of a dogmatic organization or dictatorship.

Marxism as a philosophical system is highly complex. This is natural for a doctrine that attempts to interrelate all aspects of human experience. Furthermore, considerable variation crept into the theory during the half-century in which Karl Marx and Friedrich Engels were working it out. On top of this, Marxism has been subjected to profoundly different interpretations by different parties and factions among Marx's followers—the "orthodox" Social Democrats and the Revisionists, the Bolsheviks and the Mensheviks, the Trotskyists and the Stalinists, now the Khrushchevites and the Maoites. The observer can well wonder how so many rival groups could all really be Marxist. A Communist, of course, denies that any of the "deviators" are true Marxists, while a strictly philosophical judgment might well classify all the Communists as the true deviators. For historical purposes we must accept as a Marxist anyone who calls himself one and proceed to weigh what he actually thinks.

Another source of Marxism's complexity is the dualism inherent in the philosophy itself. It is a theory, purportedly scientific, of how history actually happens, and at the same time a program of action to make history happen in the desired way. It combines a deterministic prediction of how things are going to happen—the downfall of capitalism and the coming of the classless society through the proletarian revolution—together with the moral imperative to work and fight for the earliest possible accomplishment of the revolution. Marxism is well suited as a psychological rationale for people who feel revolutionary already, particularly the educated but alienated groups in industrially developing countries. Marxism neither creates nor guides their revolutionary thrust but only gives it a vocabulary and a faith.

The theoretical core of Marxism is the class struggle theory of history. "The history of all hitherto existing society," wrote Marx and Engels in the famous Communist Manifesto of 1848, "is the history of class struggles."

Ever since the primitive communalism of the Stone Age, according to Marx and Engels, mankind has lived in "class society," with one class holding property and governmental power and "exploiting" the masses. The particular class in power, as well as the particular forms of social organization and the prevailing modes of thought, depended largely on the nature of the economic system—what kind of resources, techniques, and property were important in the "mode of production," and what class controlled those resources. Specifically, the past forms of society which Marx saw were the "Asiatic" (bureaucratic) society, ancient slave-owning society, feudalism, and capitalism. Each system led more or less naturally to the next after the forces of production outgrew it. For the future, Marx was convinced that the capitalists or "bourgeoisie" had to give way to the classless society of "communism," because the growth of industry was generating an ever-larger and more active class of proletarians who would sooner or later overthrow the whole system of private property. "What the bourgeoisie therefore produces, above all," declared Marx and Engels in the *Manifesto*, "are its own grave-diggers. Its fall and the victory of the proletariat are equally inevitable."

On the exact nature of the future "communist" society Marx and Engels had little to say in a systematic way. They did make clear their belief that the proletarian revolution would be "the work of the proletariat itself" and that it would not come until capitalism had developed as far as it could and had bogged down in the "contradictions" of monopoly and the cycle of boom-and-bust. They occasionally spoke of the "dictatorship of the proletariat" and found a model for it in the direct democracy proclaimed by the short-lived revolutionary government of the Paris Commune in 1871. Once the resistance of the expropriated property owners was overcome, the state was supposed to "wither away."

As a partial qualification to his utopian vision of the future, Marx suggested late in his career that the "communist" society would come in two stages, a "lower" stage when people continued to earn wages in relation to their work, and a "higher" stage when all notions of private income and property would disappear. Only when this happened, Marx wrote, would society "inscribe upon its banner the motto: from each according to his abilities, to each according to his needs."

Despite Marx's political efforts in the Communist League of 1848-1852 and in the International Workingmen's Association (First International), founded in 1864, his philosophy did not have substantial influence until the 1870s. He was never popular in his adopted country, England, though England gave him his model of industrial capitalism. British socialism in the Labour Party drew largely upon native inspirations of a decidedly peaceful and democratic character.

Marx's revolutionary theories began to attract a wide following on the continent of Europe in the 1870s, above all in Germany and the other Germanic nations. Marxism's strongest appeal was, as we have suggested, to the workers and intellectuals of transitional societies experiencing the rapid changes of early industrialization. Social Democratic parties, more or less officially committed to the doctrine of Marxism, were established in most European countries in the 1870s and 1880s. An international association of socialist parties that later became known as the Second International was formed in 1889.

With this organizational success, and with the spread of the democratic right to vote, the European Marxist movement rapidly changed its character from revolutionary to democratic and gradualist. Marx and Engels, late in life, recognized the possibility of revolution by ballot, and Engels wrote in 1894: "The irony of world history turns everything upside down. We, the 'revolutionaries,' the 'rebels'—we are thriving far better on legal methods than on illegal methods and revolt."

Marx's prediction of the growing misery of the working class was disproved by the rise of productivity and living standards which industrialization made possible and by the action of the Marxist parties and trade unions themselves in winning social reforms and higher wages. By 1914 most Western Marxists accepted democratic methods, though some (the "orthodox," led by Karl Kautsky) held to the language of proletarian revolution. Others (the Revisionists, inspired by Eduard Bernstein) frankly altered their theory into a philosophy of evolutionary socialism and gradual democratic reform resembling the British approach. West Europeans who remained truly revolutionary in spirit were usually not Marxists at all, but anarcho-syndicalists (mainly in the Latin countries) who followed the "direct action" theories of Bakunin and Georges Sorel.

Marxism reached Russia as a major intellectual influence rather late, in the 1890s, though Russian was the first foreign language into which *Das Kapital* was translated (1872), passing the censor because it seemed so dull. The acknowledged founder of Russian Marxism was Georgi Plekhanov, a former Populist of gradualist persuasion who fled Russia in 1881, settled in Switzerland, and discovered the philosophical attractions of Marx's theory of proletarian revolution. Thanks to popularization by Plekhanov and his followers, Marxism became widely known in Russia in the 1890s. It was intellectually attractive because it recognized the new burst of Russian industrial capitalism as a progressive force that would yet lead to revolution. The Marxists, resting their hopes on a two-stage future—bourgeois revolution followed some time later by proletarian—entered into bitter polemics with the Populists, who regarded the onset of capitalism as a disaster. As a matter of fact, Plekhanov and his followers were more Marxist than Marx, for they insisted that the country had to undergo the whole development of capitalism, while Marx had conceded that the Populists might be right about a direct transition in Russia from "feudalism" to socialism.

An actual Marxist party did not exist in Russia until the founding of the Social Democratic Party in 1898. Because of police repression

ın Russia, most of the party's initial activity was confined to the
émigrés who had fled to the West. The first real party congress was
the second, in 1903, convened in Brussels but forced to move to
London for most of its work.

It is symptomatic of émigré politics that the first major gathering
of Russian Social Democrats saw the movement split. The moving
force in this cleavage was the man destined to lead the Russian Revolution to its final form and to place his personal stamp upon the
politics of half the world, Vladimir Ilyich Ulyanov, later known by
his revolutionary pseudonym, N. Lenin. (The N stood for *nothing*.
He never called himself Nikolai, a journalistic invention of 1917 that
has refused to die.) Lenin brought to the Second Congress of the
Social Democratic Party a new concept of what the party should be
—or rather, an old, pre-Marxist concept. He spelled out this view in
his extremely important but often neglected book of 1902, *What Is
To Be Done*. Lenin presumed the party to be a willful instrument of
revolution, as the older Russian conspirators had thought, with a
premium on discipline, secrecy, and doctrinal purity. It was not to be
a mass group of the workers and any other sympathizers, but a narrow group of "professional revolutionaries" who would bring "revolutionary consciousness" to the workers "from without, that is, only
from outside of the economic struggle, from outside of the sphere of
relations between workers and employers." Where Marx had presumed that the motive force of the proletarian revolution would be
the experience of the workers themselves under capitalism, Lenin
had no faith in the revolutionary potential of the working masses
unless they were awakened and organized by the doctrinally enlightened and morally committed members of the Russian intelligentsia.
In sum, the implicit philosophy which Lenin offered to the Russian
Social Democrats was the old conspiratorial Populism dressed up in
dogmatic Marxist language.

Lenin's doctrine of the party was quickly disavowed by every Marxist leader of stature both in Russia and in the West. Nevertheless, in
the parliamentary maneuvers that ended the 1903 congress Lenin was
briefly able to command a majority, and he seized upon the Russian
term *bolsheviki* ("men of the majority") to designate his faction,
small though it actually was. His rivals in the movement, called by him
mensheviki, or minority, were really much stronger than he until the
actual revolutionary upsurge of 1917. Nominally, the two factions
remained in one party until 1912, when the Bolsheviks broke all organizational ties with the Mensheviks and claimed for themselves the
exclusive truth of Marxism.

Following his 1903 split with the rest of the Social Democrats, Lenin worked to build up an organization under his firm personal control, even if this required purging of lieutenants who had too much of a mind of their own. Doctrinally, Lenin revealed his impatient attachment to revolution as an end in itself by contriving reasons to explain why the party of the proletariat (i.e., his own party of professional revolutionaries) should *not* have to wait for the complete development of capitalism and bourgeois government in Russia. The Russian bourgeoisie, Lenin argued, was too weak and cowardly to carry out its own revolution; therefore the workers' party, with peasant support, would have to achieve the "bourgeois" revolution itself, create a "democratic dictatorship of the proletariat and peasantry," and hold power until economic progress made possible the introduction of real socialism. Some such reasoning has been the rationale of Communist movements and governments in Asia and in underdeveloped countries everywhere, even though the presumption of "proletarian" political power in the absence of socialized industry profoundly contradicts the essentials of Marxism. Here again we are compelled to note how the appeal of Marxist doctrine is not logical but psychological, with an inherent need to suppress the criticism that might expose the discrepancies between dogma and reality.

Toward the Collapse of Tsarism

Sometime in the nineteenth century—it is hard to specify with exactness—the tension between the Russian government and Russian society came to a point when the government lost the capacity to reform itself in tempo with the demands of society. Perhaps it was 1825, perhaps 1881, some might even say 1911, after which time the monarchy responded to social change only by stubbornly postponing the day of reckoning. By 1900 revolutionary stirrings of Russia-in-transition were patently obvious. Nearly everyone was against the existing government. The government knew it but yielded to no one.

Such was the revolutionary situation when in 1904 an unsuccessful military involvement nearly shook the house of tsarism to its foundations. Russian imperialism, following the path of least resistance into the Far East, where lay the helpless body of the Chinese Empire, had challenged the pretensions of a more effective foe, the newly westernized Japanese Empire. Japan attacked and decimated the Russian naval and military forces which had established themselves in Manchuria. By the time President Theodore Roosevelt of the United States arranged peace between Japan and Russia, the whole of Russian society had erupted into a state of near revolution. In this

Revolution of 1905, and in every other political upheaval of reform or revolution in modern Russia, military defeat of the Tsar's forces was the trigger.

The Revolution of 1905 commenced with the Bloody Sunday massacre of January 9 (22), when Cossacks and police attacked a protest demonstration of workers in St. Petersburg. This was the signal for a wave of demonstrations and strikes all over the country which by summer included peasant uprisings and naval mutinies. In October a general strike was proclaimed under the leadership of the St. Petersburg Council (soviet) of Workers' Deputies, whose leading figure was a youthful Menshevik, Leon Trotsky. Confronted with the prospect of complete overthrow, Tsar Nicholas II took the advice of his realistic Minister of Finance, Count Sergei Witte. In the so-called October Manifesto Nicholas promised Russia a constitution, civil liberties, and an elected parliament, the Duma.

The October Manifesto and its promises saved the monarchy by dividing the revolutionaries. Moderates and liberals were content with the proposed reform and the prospect of gradual future progress it implied. Revolutionaries of a socialist stripe—the Social Democrats and the Socialist Revolutionaries—denounced the constitutional settlement as a fraud and called for the violent overthrow of the Tsar altogether. The upshot was a final test of revolutionary strength— armed insurrection in Moscow in December 1905, bloodily put down by the regular troops lately released from the fighting in Manchuria.

The following year order was restored throughout the country, with the roundup of revolutionary leaders and pacification of the peasants by courts-martial. Nevertheless, the promised constitution, with some modifications, was put into effect. Legislative power was vested in two houses, the Duma and the Council of State. The Duma was to be elected by nearly universal manhood suffrage, but with a class basis of representation that favored property owners. The Council of State, the old advisory body largely appointed by the Tsar, was made the upper house and given a legislative veto over the Duma. Executive power, foreign policy, and military authority remained hereditary prerogatives of the Tsar and his ministers, who were responsible only to him. The new semiconstitutional monarchy in Russia resembled Imperial Germany and Japan. Like them, and like every other attempt in history to set up such a mixed constitution— England in 1660 and France in 1815, for instance—the semiconstitutional system in Russia led directly to political impasse and revolution.

The Duma elected in 1906 was boycotted by the socialists, but it still proved to have an antigovernmental majority, dominated by Paul Miliukov and the Constitutional Democrats. This First Duma was soon dissolved, only to be followed by the more radical Second Duma with Social Democratic participation. Thereupon, in 1907, Nicholas's new Prime Minister, Peter Stolypin, dissolved the Second Duma and by decree—his so-called coup d'état—altered the electoral law to give the conservatives more representation and assure a progovernment majority. From this time on the Duma was largely a docile instrument of the government, though until 1914 the revolutionaries could still get a few men into it and use it as a sounding board.

Until he was assassinated in 1911, Stolypin was the strong man in a virtually restored absolutism. During his years of office Russia experienced a new boom of capitalist industrialization, while the revolutionary parties and the labor movement were hobbled by the police. To win support for the government, Stolypin determined to facilitate individual farming by the more prosperous peasants—"a wager on the strong and sober," as he termed it. He put legislation through the Duma that allowed these people to get out of the village commune, where each farmer worked scattered strips of land, and to receive equivalent land in one compact farm. By the time of the Revolution some two million peasants had availed themselves of this opportunity. Together with the already independent peasants in the south of European Russia and in Siberia, these people constituted the kulak class with whom the Communists had to contend in the 1920s.

Stolypin's assassination, probably encouraged by reactionaries at court and in the police who hated his modest reforms, was symptomatic of the kind of action that had repeatedly thrown Russia off the path of effective peaceful reform. Affairs of state now fell under the most corrupt and degenerate influences, particularly with the ascendancy of the Siberian peasant hypnotist Grigory Rasputin. Rasputin won the confidence of the Empress Alexandra because of his apparent ability to alleviate the symptoms of hemophilia which afflicted the sovereign's only son and heir. Alexandra in turn dominated her weak husband, and Rasputin in effect was able to dictate key decisions and appointments.

In 1912 the revolutionary movement began to revive, largely in the spontaneous protests of miners and factory workers. By 1914 a major strike wave was in progress, and the experience of 1905 seemed about to begin again. Only the advent of war in August 1914, with its initial fever of patriotism and the excuse it afforded for strict policing, put a damper on the revolutionary forces. In a longer perspective, however, Russia's involvement in World War I proved to be the fatal accident that paralyzed the old regime and released all the pent-up forces of social revolution.

The war of 1914-1918, with all the disasters that followed in its train, was partly the responsibility of the Russian monarchical system itself. The Russian monarchy, like the German and Austrian, was free to make foreign policy without reference to public opinion. As Joseph Schumpeter has suggested in his essay "The Sociology of Imperialism," the policy of eager imperialism which all these governments pursued was a reflection of old monarchical, feudal, and militaristic impulse rather than any expression of the popular will or real economic interest. It is noteworthy that there has never in the whole of history been a war exclusively between two genuinely popular democracies; tribal chiefs, kings, or dictators have always been involved on one side or the other.

The great concern of the Russian government before 1914 was to preserve its influence in the Balkans in the face of Austrian pressure. Rivalry with Austria had turned Russia against Austria's ally, the German Empire. In the manner of traditional power politics Russia made an alliance with Germany's enemy, the French Republic, despite the vast differences in political principle between Russia and France. Great Britain was drawn into the Triple Entente with France and Russia in 1907, after an Anglo-Russian agreement had settled their differences in the Middle East and left half of Persia in the Russian sphere of influence.

How Russia's Balkan ambitions drew the whole of Europe into what was expected to be a brief, face-saving war is a familiar story: the assassination of the Austrian Archduke and heir to the throne, Franz Ferdinand, by Serbian nationalists; the Austrian attempt to use this as the excuse to make Russia's protégé Serbia into an Austrian satellite; Serbian resistance that presumed the backing of Russia and France; Austria's declaration of a little punitive war, with the assurance of German support; and the outbreak of general hostilities between the two great alliance systems, German-Austrian and Russian-French-British. As in 1904, the war was more welcomed than feared by the Russian authorities with respect to its internal effect on the stability of the government.

Germany's strategy when the war began was to overwhelm the French first, and the Russians were able to take the offensive on the Eastern front, until they met a crushing defeat in the Battle of Tannenberg (September 1914). In 1915 the Germans threw their main effort eastward and again trounced the Russian armies. The Russians were forced to evacuate all of Russian Poland and Lithuania and fell back to a line approximating the Russo-Polish boundary of 1921-1939. Here the front remained stabilized until the Revolution of 1917.

The cost of the war in every sense—financial, economic, manpower, morale—proved to be more than the tsarist regime could bear. Fearful of sharing authority with representatives of the population, the bureaucracy scorned the War Industry Committees which united all classes, and thus threw away the reservoir of patriotic sentiment that the government had enjoyed in 1914. The economy was badly mismanaged: the army was overmobilized and undersupplied, with a surplus of draftees waiting in city garrisons and a shortage of men working in factories and farms. The railroad system began to deteriorate. The state vodka monopoly was supplanted by nation-wide prohibition, so that the state lost its liquor revenue to the bootleggers. The government's wartime deficit was covered by the printing press, with the inevitable result of inflation. Prices rose faster than wages, and even the available food could not be transported to the city consumers in adequate quantity. The whole nation stirred uneasily.

At the top the policies and personnel of the tsarist government revealed even greater incompetence as the war went on. This was especially so after Nicholas II went to Headquarters at Mogilev on the Dniepr in 1915 to take personal command of his troops and left the government in the hands of Alexandra, Rasputin, and a succession of stupid ministers. The Duma, after first trying to help, was able only to oppose. In January 1917 it was dissolved altogether, and the Revolution of February found only an unofficial committee of Duma leaders in Petrograd to take charge of events. Meanwhile, in December 1916, Rasputin had been boldly assassinated by a conspiracy of nobles. The institution of the monarchy, though brittle and unyielding, was fast crumbling in the face of internal decay and mass disaffection. Underlying and precipitating causes had coincided. The stage was set for revolution.

1917

Though revolutionaries had been plotting and agitating in Russia for nearly a century, the actual fall of the Tsar was, ironically enough, totally unplanned and spontaneous. Neither this event nor its consequences were expected by the revolutionaries; Lenin was writing just a month before that revolution might never come in his lifetime. Even the Bolshevik coup of October 1917 proves on close examination to have been more muddle than plan.

A rash of strikes and food riots in Petrograd was the occasion for the February Revolution; crowds got out of hand, army units refused to fire, and the police power broke down. Literally overnight, between February 26 and February 27 (March 11-12), the tsarist government lost its authority. The magic spell that commanded mass obedience was dissipated when enough people were willing to be shot at, and as a result the abstraction known as the government simply ceased to exist.

The vacuum left by the collapse of tsarist order was filled quickly but only partially. In the manner of earlier social revolutions, every form of radical impulse and mass defiance of authority soon erupted all over the country. For the time being a nominal ruling authority was proclaimed in Petrograd by a self-appointed committee of members of the dissolved Duma. These moderate or conservative representatives of that class-biased body formed a cabinet—the Provisional Government—and took over direction of the imperial ministries. The Prime Minister, Prince Georgi Lvov, was only a figurehead, and the real leadership was exercised by Miliukov, the Kadet chief, as Minister of Foreign Affairs and Alexander Guchkov, a constitutional monarchist, as Minister of War. Civil liberties for the whole nation were proclaimed, but in fact there was no longer any power that could curb popular liberty.

Simultaneously with the formation of the Provisional Government, the socialist underground leaders in Petrograd revived the old 1905 institution of a workers' council or soviet. They went to the factories and barracks in the city and got themselves democratically elected, along with many ordinary workers and soldiers. Similar soviets were quickly formed in every other major Russian city and in many rural districts, while the Petrograd Soviet assumed national leadership of the movement. The soviets gained considerable de facto governmental power, since the masses of workers, soldiers, and peasants had more contact with them than with the Provisional Government. Formally, however, the soviets decided to acknowledge the temporary authority of the Provisional Government, "insofar as" it did not harm the Revolution.

At first the most crucial problem for the Provisional Government was foreign policy, and particularly the question on what terms to continue the war against the Central Powers. Most Russian opinion, including that of the soviets, inclined toward some form of negotiated peace, "without annexations and without indemnities." Some conservative and moderate leaders, notably Foreign Minister Miliukov, wanted to fight the war to a finish for the sake of imperialist expan-

sion to the Straits. The upshot was the mob protests of the April
Days of 1917, the resignation of Miliukov, and the reorganization of
the Provisional Government.

The new cabinet of May 1917 was a coalition of former Provisional
Government ministers and members of the Petrograd Soviet (who
came, however, without firm endorsement by the Soviet). Lvov remained as Prime Minister; Miliukov was replaced as Foreign Minister
by another Kadet, Mikhail Tereshchenko. The strong man in the new
cabinet was Alexander Kerensky, a moderate socialist lawyer who had
been Minister of Justice in the Provisional Government and who now
moved up to become Minister of War.

Kerensky was determined to show Russia's allies that the country
could still fight, and in late June 1917 he ordered an offensive against
the Germans on the dormant eastern front. The offensive was a total
failure, and the Russian troops, disorganized by the decay of military
discipline since the February Revolution, were thrown back in utter
disarray. From this time on the army disintegrated rapidly in a wave
of desertions and mutinies. By the time of the October Revolution
it had nearly ceased to exist as an effective fighting force. Meanwhile
the Provisional Government was shaken by violent riots—the so-called
July Days—in which the Bolsheviks were feeling out their new revolutionary potential.

The sequel to the July Days was another reorganization of the
Provisional Government. Kerensky now became Prime Minister, with
a cabinet about equally divided between the old Duma politicians
on the one hand and Mensheviks and Right Socialist Revolutionaries
from the Soviet on the other. However, as the original leaders of the
Soviet gained more influence within the cabinet, they were losing
ground in their own constituency. Because of the ultrademocratic
practice of unrestricted recall and re-election of deputies, the more
moderate members of the soviets were being replaced by more radical
men. Popular support for the Bolshevik Party, with its allies, the Left
Socialist Revolutionaries, rapidly increased. By the beginning of September 1917 the Bolsheviks had a majority in the key soviets of
Petrograd and Moscow. Thus, the upsurge of mass revolutionary feeling set the stage for a Bolshevik Party take-over.

At the time of the February Revolution the Bolshevik Party was
a weak and leaderless underground movement of less than 25,000
members, considerably inferior to the Mensheviks and moreover inclined to cooperate with them. The Provisional Government's blanket
amnesty for political offenders allowed the Bolshevik leaders to return

to Petrograd from exile in Siberia or outside the country. Even so, under the direction of Joseph Stalin and Leo Kamenev, the Bolsheviks at first went along with the other parties in the soviets in supporting the Provisional Government and a defensive war. They subscribed to the Menshevik interpretation of Marxism, viewing the Provisional Government as a bourgeois regime that would facilitate the growth of capitalism—thought to be a prerequisite to an eventual proletarian revolution.

Lenin and most of the other Bolshevik intellectuals were abroad when the Tsar fell. They took at once a radical stand against the Provisional Government and hastened to return to Russia to promote further revolution. Lenin secured permission from the German government to cross from Switzerland to Scandinavia and proceeded via Finland to Petrograd. Immediately upon his arrival he launched into a tirade against the Provisional Government—his so-called April Theses—and threw his own party, not to mention the rest of the soviet leaders, into consternation. Lenin called, in effect, for the overthrow of the Provisional Government by the soviets and for international revolution against all the warring "imperialist" governments on both sides.

Lenin's first task was to persuade his own party that Russia was ready for the proletarian revolution. In the span of a month or two, by intense personal pressure, he had won a majority of the Bolshevik leaders to his new line of "All Power to the Soviets." He was aided in this reorientation by the shift of numerous left-wing Mensheviks (including Trotsky) to the Bolshevik ranks and by the rapid increase in the party's rank-and-file membership (to around 100,000 by October). Nevertheless, a substantial minority of overcautious Bolshevik leaders continued to drag their feet. Until the very day of the October Revolution Lenin was unsure of the party's resoluteness concerning his goal.

The demonstrations of the July Days caused a temporary setback for the Bolsheviks, who were accused of trying to overthrow the government and, moreover, of being in the pay of the Germans.* The Bolshevik Party was outlawed and some of its leaders were jailed,

---

* The charge that the Bolsheviks were German agents was a major point in anti-Bolshevik opinion both in Russia and among the Western allies. This suggests how far wartime nationalism surpassed antirevolutionary feeling as a determining political emotion. In actuality, the Bolsheviks, like many other groups, almost certainly got some of the funds that the Germans were scattering about in Russia to encourage dissension. On the other hand, there is no evidence that Bolshevik opinion or action was in any way under German control.

while Lenin fled to the legally separate jurisdiction of Finland to escape arrest. The Bolsheviks were nonetheless able to hold a congress and expand their influence among the workers.

An event that irreparably upset the precarious equilibrium of Kerensky's government was the abortive right-wing coup attempted in late August by the army's new commander-in-chief, General Lavr Kornilov. Though appointed by Kerensky, Kornilov quickly won the support of the political Right, from the Kadets over to the monarchists, as the man who could disband the soviets, restore order, and stop the trend of the Revolution to the left. When his efforts to effect such a change by negotiating with Kerensky broke down, he ordered his most reliable Cossack units to march on Petrograd. This time it was the Left—including the practically relegalized Bolsheviks —who rallied to defend the government, and Kornilov's forces deserted the cause of counterrevolution. Kornilov was ousted from his command and placed under arrest, though he remained in the wings to assume leadership of the anti-Communist Whites in 1918. But Kerensky had lost the confidence of both Right and Left, and the Bolsheviks surged ahead to win control of the soviets.

This political advance by the Bolsheviks was the manifestation of profound revolutionary currents that were sweeping the country. Economic conditions grew steadily worse, with inflation and the breakdown of the railroads. The industrial working class, who were in a majority in the major cities, repudiated the property rights and factory discipline of private capitalism. Increasingly frequent strikes contributed further to the general economic disorder. New factory committees, usually more radical and pro-Bolshevik than the trade unions, tried to assert direct authority over their plants in a spontaneous movement toward workers' control.

Lenin did no more than endorse this movement when he wrote in *State and Revolution*:

> It is quite possible, after the overthrow of the capitalists and the bureaucrats, to proceed immediately, overnight, to supersede them in the *control* of production and distribution. . . .

> The workers, having conquered political power, will smash the old bureaucratic apparatus, they will shatter it to its very foundations, they will destroy it to the very roots; and they will replace it by a new one, consisting of the very same workers and office employees, *against* whose transformation into bureaucrats the measures will at once be taken which were specified by Marx and Engels: (1) not only election, but also recall at any time; (2) pay not exceeding that of a workman;

(3) immediate introduction of control and supervision by *all*, so that *all* shall become "bureaucrats" for a time and that, therefore, *nobody* may be able to become a "bureaucrat."

This vision should not be taken as a firm guideline of Lenin's future policy. *State and Revolution*, which Lenin wrote while hiding in Finland in the late summer and early fall of 1917, was really propaganda. Though it is still regarded by Communist and anti-Communist alike as the basic statement of Lenin's political theory, the book has served more as window dressing than as plan for Communist political practice.

Another vast revolutionary force was the peasant movement of the summer and fall of 1917. The peasants had been hungry for more land ever since the Emancipation of 1861, and their increasing numbers aggravated their discontent. The Provisional Government promised a land reform, but the legislative details were delayed. The peasants grew impatient, and with the general breakdown of authority and discipline throughout Russian society they began to take matters into their own hands and seize the landlords' estates by force.

At the time of the October Revolution the Russian countryside was in the turmoil of spontaneous revolt which the Bolsheviks merely ratified. In turn, the Bolsheviks won substantial peasant support— directly in some places but more often through their allies, the Left Socialist Revolutionaries. These Left SR's were the heirs of the direct-action tradition of the old Populist movement. They split off from the moderates of that party in 1917, much as the Bolsheviks had split away from the Menshevik Social Democrats in 1903. Though the Left SR's were non-Marxists, differing profoundly from the Bolsheviks in matters of theory, the two groups were closely akin in revolutionary fervor. The Left SR's threw their support to the Bolsheviks in the crucial days of the October Revolution and in the first months of the Soviet regime and thus proved to be of crucial assistance to Bolshevik victory.

A third revolutionary social force of 1917, of even more decisive immediate significance than the workers and peasants, was the army. In the army more than anywhere else the rebellion of the Russian people against the authority of the old order and its representatives was manifest. One of the first acts of the Petrograd Soviet was to issue, without any authority whatsoever, Order Number One sanctioning the election of democratic soldiers' committees. Discipline crumbled, while representatives of all the Left parties went to the troops with the promise of peace. Following the June offensive and the July Days the army began to disintegrate physically despite Kerensky's restoration of the prerevolutionary death penalty for desertion. The soldiers—peasant conscripts, for the most part—began to "vote with their feet," to make their way homeward and join in the land seizures.

In this ferment of revolution the army was in no condition to resist the Germans, as the latter proved in several probing actions on the Baltic coast. The Provisional Government began to contemplate moving away from Petrograd, a thought that led all the parties in the Soviet to believe and to charge that the conservatives wanted to turn the city over to the Germans in order to stifle the Revolution. At the same time, the Russian High Command prepared to move reserve troops to the front from the large city garrisons, especially from Petrograd. These reservists, whom the Revolution had made virtually immune to transfer and combat, had less stomach for the war than the front-line troops, and the prospect of duty in the trenches made them all the more responsive to the unqualified peace appeal of the most uncompromising revolutionary party, the Bolsheviks. Disaffected army units proved to be the key force at the Bolsheviks' disposal when the time came to seize power.

The Kornilov episode and its aftermath of Bolshevik political gain brought Lenin to his decision. From Finland he wrote a secret message to the Bolshevik Central Committee in Petrograd:

> Having obtained a majority in the Soviets of Workers' and Soldiers deputies of both capitals [Petrograd and Moscow], the Bolsheviks can and must take governmental power into their hands . . . It would be naïve to wait for a "formal" majority on the side of the Bolsheviks; no revolution ever waits for *this*. . . . History will not forgive us if we do not assume power now.

Surprisingly, the Petrograd leaders of the Bolshevik Party were so concerned with keeping their collective head above the political waters that they voted to disregard Lenin's instructions altogether and nearly destroyed the message. Though Lenin reiterated in letter after letter his demand for revolutionary action, the Central Committee continued to avoid the question until early October. By this time Lenin had won more backing and the Central Committee decided to have him come to Petrograd secretly to discuss the issue with them. Lenin did so, and in the crucial meeting on the night of October 10-11, after hours of unrecorded debate, he succeeded in getting the Committee's endorsement of his resolution declaring that the political situation "places the armed uprising on the order of the day."

Verbal acceptance by the party leadership of Lenin's demand for insurrection did not guarantee the end of opposition or the implementation of the plan. Vehement opposition was voiced by Kamenev and by Grigory Zinoviev, who had been displaced by Trotsky as Lenin's first lieutenant and had gone over to the right-wing opposition. Zinoviev and Kamenev circulated a memorandum to the Bolshevik Party which declared in part: "We have never said that the Russian working class *alone,* by its own forces, would be able to bring the present revolution to a victorious conclusion. . . . Before history, before the international proletariat, before the Russian Revolution and the Russian working class, we have no right to stake the whole future on the card of an armed uprising." It is ironic that the most clearly Marxist reasoning in the Bolshevik debate on the insurrection was directed *against* Lenin's plan to seize power.

On October 17 the Zinoviev-Kamenev statement was picked up by the non-Bolshevik press, and now the Petrograd public knew what everyone had suspected: that the Bolsheviks were considering some sort of "move" against the Provisional Government. Lenin reacted with a furious barrage of letters and articles attacking the "strikebreaking" activity of Zinoviev and Kamenev. So preoccupied were the Bolshevik leaders over this matter of party unity that they failed to make any substantial plans for insurrection.*

The documentation or absence of documentation regarding these days suggests that most of the Bolshevik leadership, including Trotsky and Stalin, were afraid to risk an uprising. Though they were reluctant to oppose Lenin openly, they were evidently content to wait for the national revolutionary forum of the Second Congress of Soviets on October 20, which they hoped would vote them into power. They did take steps to get control of the Petrograd military garrison through the agency of the Military Revolutionary Committee set up under the Petrograd Soviet. However, the thought uppermost in this effort was to prevent a second Kornilovite coup that might be effected by transferring the revolutionary garrison out of Petrograd or by surrendering the city to the Germans.

There was much delay in getting the Military Revolutionary Com-

---

* The following account of the October Revolution may strike the reader as a departure from the familiar views of both Communist and non-Communist historians. It is based on an intensive research project by this writer, the conclusions of which were outlined in a paper to the American Historical Association in December 1961.

mittee into action. Only the decision of the Mensheviks and Right SR's to postpone the Congress of the Soviets from the 20th to the 25th preserved for the Bolsheviks the opportunity to strike before the Congress. By October 22 the Military Revolutionary Committee ventured to declare, in the interest of "the defense of revolutionary order against counterrevolutionary attempts," that "no orders to the garrison are valid unless signed by the Military Revolutionary Committee." This was the real revolutionary step, when the Bolsheviks and Left SR's of the Soviet usurped military authority and made themselves a *de facto* government vastly superior in power to Kerensky's authority in the Winter Palace.

The Provisional Government under Kerensky had been losing support steadily since the Kornilov affair. The Kadets, not to mention the monarchists and the military, had lost all regard for Kerensky and were prepared to support a military take-over. There is reason to believe that Kerensky's military commander in Petrograd, Colonel Polkovnikov, was deceiving him about the actual danger of the Bolsheviks, in the thought that a Bolshevik blow at Kerensky would open the door for a right-wing countercoup. Kerensky had also lost the support of the Mensheviks and many of the SR's. On the very eve of the Bolshevik take-over Kerensky lost a vote of confidence in his own provisional parliament, the Council of the Republic, on the land issue and peace issue.

As his position crumbled, Kerensky determined to strike a preventive blow at the Bolsheviks, who still underestimated their own strength and were waiting for the Congress of Soviets. In the early morning hours of October 24 government troops took up strategic positions in the city and closed the Bolshevik newspapers. This was the signal for emergency countermeasures by the Bolsheviks in the Soviet headquarters at the Smolny Institute. The Red Guards of armed factory workers and pro-Bolshevik army units were called out to defend the Soviet. Their defense was unexpectedly successful; the government forces melted away. By the evening of October 24 the Bolsheviks controlled most of the city.

There was still no plan; no document of a plan, date, or call for the insurrection has ever been produced. Lenin, hiding in the working-class district of Petrograd north of the Neva River, was still ignorant of the course of events. He wrote on the evening of the 24th: "It is as clear as can be that delaying the uprising now really means death. . . . It would be a disaster or formalism to wait for the uncertain voting of October 25. The people have a right and a duty to decide such questions not by voting but by force. . . ." Toward midnight Lenin heard of the fighting and took a streetcar to Smolny. All was in confusion there, and Lenin evidently assumed that his earlier orders were actually being carried out. Official Soviet history has never indicated the contrary, though the improvisations and delays in the Bolshevik attack on the government testify to the accidental and unplanned nature of the action.

Calls finally went out early in the morning of the 25th to the Bolshevik forces at the Baltic naval bases. The railroad stations and communications centers in Petrograd were occupied, and military forces were assembled to attack the last stronghold of the Provisional Government, the Winter Palace itself. Resistance was negligible, but it took all day on the 25th and into the early hours of the 26th before the revolutionaries managed to occupy the palace and put an end to the Provisional Government. Kerensky himself slipped away on the morning of the 25th, and after a vain attempt to bring troops from the front against the Bolsheviks, he fled the country.

When the Second Congress of Soviets opened near midnight on the 25th, a fortuitous chain of circumstances enabled the Bolsheviks to present it with what Lenin had demanded: the *de facto* Bolshevik possession of power and the foundations of a one-party dictatorship baptized in blood. Success, as so often happens, came to the Bolsheviks not so much by reason of their power, wisdom, chicanery, or determination (though they profited by all these) as by the greater weakness, confusion, and disunity of all the rival contenders for power. It is a law of revolution that the best-organized extremists take power and end anarchy. In the Russian situation it did not require much organization to be best.

There are, of course, a number of obvious factors which must be given their due in explaining the political success of the Bolsheviks. Without Lenin's personality—his undeviating drive for power, his tactical shrewdness, his ability to browbeat all opposition—there would have been no Bolshevik Party, let alone a party capable of seizing and holding power in a crisis. Organization there was too, superior to that of the other parties, though far less disciplined and effective than the image of the subsequent Communist Party leads the historian to assume. In part, the Bolsheviks won simply because they were the most radical, the party most in tune with the radicalism of Russian society in 1917, the party most ready to abandon scruples about legality, property, and obligations to one's allies. Theirs was the simplest and hence most effective propaganda: "Bread, Land, and Peace," "All Power to the Soviets."

It is natural to try to assign to such a decisive event as the Bolshevik Revolution powerful and irresistible causes, or at least a master plan. Careful study suggests that neither of these approaches is valid, that the Bolshevik Revolution did not *have* to happen, that in fact it was a freak accident, throwing Russia's subsequent development on a track very different from what it might have been, for better or for worse. But whatever the alternative track, it is hard to imagine that it could have been for Russia in the conditions of 1917 anything but one of revolutionary or counterrevolutionary extremism.

The Revolution and the Soviet System

The Russian Revolution was not over when the Bolsheviks stumbled into power. Revolutionary flux and violence worsened, and the struggle of revolutionary against counterrevolutionary did not come to an end until 1921. For its first three and a half years the new government of the soviets lived in the midst of revolutionary turmoil and took its permanent shape from the conditions of that turmoil.

Legally speaking, all the October Revolution did was to make the unofficial government of the soviets the official government. This claim was, endorsed by the Second Congress of Soviets, which also gave its assent to the new executive cabinet created by the revolutionaries, the Council of People's Commissars, replacing Kerensky's Provisional Government. Lenin, naturally, became Chairman of the Council or Prime Minister. Trotsky took the next most important post, Commissar of Foreign Affairs. Military affairs, in keeping with the collective spirit, were put under a committee. Stalin, because of his Georgian background, was brought in as Commissar of Nationalities.

In theory, the soviets were supposed to be the ultimate organs of direct revolutionary democracy. The Congress and through it the central organs of government were therefore elected by the local soviets, not by the worker and peasant voters directly. "Exploiters" were excluded from voting altogether. Executive and legislative power were thought to be fused, not separated, and merely delegated from the local soviets to the periodic Congresses and thence to the permanent central organs. The place of a central legislature was taken by the Central Executive Committee of the Soviets, a body created in mid-1917. The CEC in turn delegated day-to-day responsibility to the Council of People's Commissars. All of these arrangements were formalized in the constitution of the Russian Socialist Federated Soviet Republic approved by the Congress of Soviets in mid-1918.

Technically, all these soviet bodies were still open to any of the parties which had taken part in the soviets during 1917, but the

Right SR's and most of the Mensheviks walked out of the Second Congress of Soviets in protest against the Bolsheviks' violent assumption of power. The Congress and the Central Executive Committee were left overwhelmingly under the domination of the Bolsheviks and the Left SR's. The Council of People's Commissars could expect automatic ratification of its actions and began at once to govern by decree.

The Bolshevik leaders themselves at first disagreed about the nature of the revolutionary government. Those who had actively or tacitly resisted the idea of insurrection now came out for the principle of a coalition cabinet representing all parties in the soviets. Negotiations to this end were actually carried on for some days, but the idea met with too much resistance from both political extremes. The Right SR's and many Mensheviks refused to enter any cabinet including Lenin and Trotsky, while Lenin and Trotsky sought to discredit all the non-Bolsheviks. The idea of a broad coalition was bound to fail, and when the Council of People's Commissars issued decrees aiming to silence opposition newspapers, the cautious wing of the Bolsheviks rebelled against Lenin and resigned from the Central Committee. "We cannot assume responsibility," they declared, "for this ruinous policy of the Central Committee, carried out against the will of a large part of the proletariat and soldiers, who crave the earliest cessation of bloodshed between the separate parts of the democratic forces." All that survived of the coalition idea was the inclusion of three Left SR's in the Council of People's Commissars, while a few Mensheviks and independents provided the only "loyal opposition," so to speak, in the Central Executive Committee.

The initial steps of the new Bolshevik government were more a matter of talk than of action. Decrees concerning land and workers' control gave recognition to the mass revolution in the countryside and in the factories. Equality was promised to national minorities; the Orthodox Church was officially separated from the state; legal class distinctions were abolished. A decree on peace called for immediate negotiations to end the war and threatened to unleash revolution against any government that held back. A crowning measure of insult to Russia's allies was the publication of the secret treaties which the tsarist government had signed in anticipation of a division of the spoils of war.

The new government of the soviets faced immense practical difficulties in consolidating its power. In Petrograd there was a brief strike by government employees. In many parts of the country it was some time before the local soviets actually wrested power from the authorities loyal to the Provisional Government, and in Moscow there was a week of bloody fighting before the Bolsheviks prevailed. In the south, in the Ukraine and the Cossack region, the new regime did not succeed in establishing its authority at all. Economically, Lenin contented himself with the policy of "one foot in socialism." For the time being he nationalized only the banks and left it to the workers' control movement to curb the power of private industry.

The socialist policies and the political dictatorship of the Bolshevik Party developed only by stages, without any very clear plan. Conceivably, the political structure of soviet government could have permitted a separation of powers and the interplay of majority and opposition, as it did to some extent in the first few months. The trouble was that neither the Bolshevik leadership nor the SR and Menshevik moderates were willing to share power with the other side, not to mention the conservatives and the military who were biding their time until an opportunity came to overthrow the soviets altogether.

The extent of such opposition, together with the Bolsheviks' dictatorial proclivities, led the Bolsheviks in December 1917 to take the fateful step of reviving that mainstay of tsarist rule, the secret political police. Under the soviets it was the Extraordinary Commission to Combat Counterrevolutionary Activities, or Cheka, from its Russian initials. The Cheka soon got power to arrest, sentence, and summarily execute suspected enemies of the regime. With slight variations in the name and powers of the police organization, this system of political control has remained in force ever since. It became the State Political Administration (GPU) in 1922, was incorporated into the People's Commissariat of Internal Affairs (NKVD) in 1934, functioned as the Ministry of Internal Affairs (MVD) or the Ministry of State Security (MGB) from 1945 to 1953, and now operates as the Committee of State Security (KGB). The police role of uprooting the sources of political dissent with secret agents and arbitrary arrest remains firmly in effect, though the actual extent of terror and killings has waned significantly since Stalin's time.

Another crucial political choice was presented to the Bolsheviks by the election of the Constituent Assembly, already scheduled by the Provisional Government in order to prepare a permanent constitution. The election, held in late November, 1917, a month after the Bolshevik take-over, was the only fair and genuine ballot that Russia has ever had. The Bolsheviks recorded their urban strength by polling some nine million votes, but this gave them only second place, far behind the peasant-based SR's with over twenty million votes. Lenin refused to accept the results, arguing that his Left SR allies were not appropriately represented among the SR candidates, but he made no effort to have new voting. Rather than risk the loss of power to the moderate peasant party, he determined to use force. The Constituent Assembly met in January 1918 for one day; the Bolshevik minority walked out, and the assembly was forcibly disbanded. This marks the real beginning of the Bolshevik dictatorship.

Apart from the consolidation of political power, the most difficult problem for the Bolsheviks during the first few months of the regime was the question of the war and how to end it. The Bolsheviks had amended the Marxist assumption of a simultaneous world-wide pro-letarian take-over by adding the old messianic notion of the Russian revolutionary tradition—that Russia in its relative backwardness could be a pure revolutionary inspiration to the advanced coun-tries of the West. Lenin saw in the horrors of World War I the necessary impetus for the international revolution and espoused as his slogan, "Turn the international war into a civil war." Trotsky, with his "Theory of Permanent Revolution," came to much the same conclusion. The idea of the war as the occasion for general revolu-tion and general revolution as the way to end the war, coupled with the sense of Russia's mission to launch the general revolution, was the theoretical rationale for the whole Bolshevik drive to power. Otherwise, it was impossible to explain a Marxist proletarian revolu-tion in Russia, where capitalism was still young.

It is important to understand the place of international theory in Bolshevik thinking in order to evaluate the idea of world revolution which has distinguished the Communist movement. The Bolsheviks assumed that they had to have world revolution in order to survive in Russia. The question between the two Bolshevik wings in 1917 was whether Russian example and encouragement could bring on that revolution, or whether the Party should play safe because of the lack of international support.

Following the October coup and the decree on peace, the Soviet government invited all the warring governments to negotiate or face revolution. Russia's allies regarded this as treachery and refused. Germany saw an immediate opportunity and commenced peace negotiations with the Russians at the town of Brest-Litovsk behind the German lines in Russian Poland. When the Russians concen-trated on propaganda, the Germans threatened to resume the war. Russia had no longer any army capable of fighting back, but the Bolshevik hotheads wanted to resist with guerrilla warfare in the be-

lief that this would evoke revolution in the West. Lenin disagreed
and surprised his followers in January 1918 by coming out for an old-
fashioned peace in which Russia would pay the German victors the
price they demanded. This suggestion touched off two months of
violent controversy in the Bolshevik ranks, with Lenin now backed by
the Zinoviev-Kamenev group as well as by Stalin and other practical-
minded people, against the left wing of Nikolai Bukharin and
Trotsky, who viewed Lenin's peace proposal as a betrayal of the
principles of the Revolution. The leftists were willing to risk the
temporary destruction of the Soviet government to make the most
of the chances for world revolution and keep their own record pure.
Some of them even contended that without international revolution
the regime in Russia would degenerate and lose the virtues of a
proletarian revolution. Left-wing critics of Soviet Russia have been
drawn to this conclusion many times since.

The debate on peace was finally resolved when the Germans resumed hostilities late in February 1918. By the narrowest of margins
Lenin won two crucial votes in the Bolshevik Central Committee:
seven to six, when Trotsky came over to his side to ask the Germans
for terms again, and (with a more nearly full attendance) seven to
four, with Trotsky's group of four abstaining, to accept the terms.
The peace was signed at Brest-Litovsk on March 3, 1918.

Under the treaty Russia lost her whole western and southern
border region, with fifty million people and the most productive
industrial, mining, and agricultural segments of her economy. Russian
Poland and the Baltic provinces stayed under German occupation,
and the Caucasus fell to the Germans and Turks, while Ukrainian
independence under a pro-German nationalist government was recognized. Meanwhile, the Soviet government recognized Finland as an
independent republic in December 1917—the only voluntary ob-
servance by the Bolsheviks of Lenin's doctrine of self-determination.

The peace of Brest-Litovsk was resisted by all of Lenin's opponents,
from the ultra-Left to the far Right. A group known as the Left
Communists led by Bukharin held talks with the equally incensed
Left SR's to plan a cabinet overturn, remove Lenin as Chairman of
the Council of People's Commissars, and resume the war. Bukharin's
group soon backed away from this rash step, but the Left SR's resigned from the cabinet and went into legal opposition. Later, their
bitterness about the peace carried them over the line into revolutionary plotting. In July 1918 they attempted a coup in Moscow
(which had become the capital in March) and assassinated the German Ambassador in the hope of provoking a resumption of the war.

The plan failed, the revolt was put down, and the Left SR's were outlawed. Thus ended the last substance of a multiparty system in Soviet Russia.

The Brest-Litovsk decision proved to be of fundamental significance in shaping the future of Soviet relations with the outside world, as well as in complicating the relationship between theory and practice for the professing Marxists in the Communist Party (as the Bolsheviks restyled themselves in 1918). Lenin defended the peace as an absolute necessity to buy time and preserve the Soviet regime. By implication this put the survival of the Soviet regime ahead of any opportunities for spreading the proletarian revolution abroad. This priority was soon rationalized by the doctrine that Soviet Russia was the citadel of world revolution, the stronghold whose existence would sustain the world revolutionary movement and whose fall would cripple the chances for proletarian revolution everywhere. Such a presumed dependence of the proletarian revolution on the power of Russia was, of course, a far cry from original Marxism. It was patently a twisting of theory to justify the Russia-first commitment of the revolutionaries who had gained power there. This commitment, whatever the strategic reversals and tactical innovations it has involved, has remained the central operating principle of Soviet foreign policy ever since.

The internal equilibrium enjoyed by the Soviet regime in the first few months of 1918 was rudely upset in May by the spread of civil war. The Czechoslovak Legion of deserters and former prisoners of war was being evacuated via the Trans-Siberian Railway and Vladivostok to France so that it could continue in the war against the Central Powers. It was strung out in trains from the Volga to the Pacific when simultaneous clashes with Soviet forces who tried to disarm them occurred in May 1918 all along the rail line, and the Czechs seized control of the railway. This was the signal for anti-Communist forces throughout the region to overthrow the local soviets and repudiate the authority of Moscow. A provisional government was set up at Samara on the Volga by Right SR members of the defunct Constituent Assembly, and officers of the old army hastily organized a "White" force to overthrow the "Red" Communist regime.

As a result of the treaty with Germany and the Czech uprising, the Soviet regime was reduced virtually to the old Muscovy of Ivan III. The revolutionary government was fighting for its life, and desperate measures were taken to create a new military force in place of the army that had dissolved during the Revolution. Trotsky was appointed Commissar of War (after resigning the Foreign Commissariat in protest over the Treaty of Brest-Litovsk) and proceeded to organize a new Workers' and Peasants' Red Army under the strictest authority and discipline. Revolutionary purists in the Communist Party protested these organizational methods and Trotsky's employment of former tsarist officers as a betrayal of revolutionary principle. But in military affairs as in foreign policy and the administration of the economy, survival soon dictated principles of action that permanently altered the nature of the Soviet system.

The Civil War in Russia, resembling in some respects the English Civil War of 1642-1646, raged for two and a half years. It was soon complicated by foreign intervention on the side of the Whites—by the British, French, Japanese, and Americans—recalling the experience of foreign intervention in the French Revolution. The Allied leaders were obsessed after Brest-Litovsk with the need to restore the Eastern front against Germany. By permission of the Soviet government, in the spring of 1918 they landed troops at Archangel on the White Sea and at Vladivostok, ostensibly to guard the Allied munitions which had been shipped to these ports. When general civil war broke out, however, the Allied forces were quickly drawn in, partly through temptation to back the Whites as enemies of Germany, partly out of the fear of Communist revolutionary influence in their own countries, and, in the case of Japan, partly out of imperialist designs on Russian territory. More important than the presence of Allied troops was the financial aid and munitions supplied to the White armies by the Allied governments.

In the face of the White threat, the Communist Party closed ranks and cracked down on all opposition in the territory under its control. Practically all non-Communists—the Right SR's, most of the Mensheviks, and (after their uprising) the Left SR's—were barred from the soviets and thus politically outlawed. This perfected the one-party Communist dictatorship in practice, though Lenin did not clearly make it part of official Soviet theory for another couple of years.

The Communist Party quickly built up an elaborate system to control the activities of the Soviets, other institutions of government, and social organizations such as the trade unions. All these bodies were considered "transmission belts" to transmit the will and doctrine of the Party to the mass of the population. The soviets, local and central, became nothing but auxiliaries to implement Party decisions. Real governmental policy was made by the Communist Central Committee, and after 1919 by the smaller Political Bureau or

Politburo. At the same time, the organizational and control functions of the Party were centralized under the Organizational Bureau (Orgburo) and the Secretariat.

The first great crisis of the Civil War came in the summer of 1918, when the Whites drove up the Volga in an attempt to capture Moscow. The abortive revolt of the Left SR's was followed by other anti-Communist uprisings on Soviet territory. In August Lenin was wounded by a would-be assassin. The Communists responded to the crisis by unleashing the Red Terror—the indiscriminate arrest and execution of counterrevolutionary suspects and hostages. The Red Terror was matched by equivalent atrocities on the part of the Whites, who in addition indulged in anti-Jewish pogroms in the manner of tsarist times. Tsar Nicholas and the royal family, already prisoners in the Urals, were liquidated by the Communists to forestall their release by the Whites.

By the fall of 1918 the Communists had met the first White drive and thrown it back. Then, in November, their situation was further relieved by the collapse of Imperial Germany and the end of World War I. This turn of events terminated the ostensible excuse for Allied intervention in Russia and permitted the Communists to push back into the southern and western border regions that had been under German occupation.

Elsewhere in Europe the end of the war seemed to have ushered in the international revolutionary crisis that the Communists were waiting for. The Russians were particularly excited by the revolution in Germany that overthrew the Kaiser and brought the Socialists to power, and by the expressions of pro-Soviet feeling that came from leftist and antiwar groups among socialists everywhere. Lenin determined to realize his dream of a new, really revolutionary International to supplant the Second International of the Socialists. In March 1919 the Russians convoked a meeting of unofficial left-wing socialist representatives from abroad and then had this meeting proclaim itself the founding Congress of the Communist International. Trotsky wrote the manifesto issued by the Congress, in which he called in the most explicit terms for violent international proletarian revolution:

> We summon the working men and women of all countries to unite under the Communist banner under which the first great victories have already been won. . . .
> Under the banner of workers' soviets, under the banner of revolutionary struggle for power and the dictatorship of the proletariat, under

the banner of the Third International, proletarians of all countries, unite!

The initial high hopes of the First Comintern Congress were not borne out, though Communists did come to power in Hungary for a few months in 1919. What this meeting and the following one in 1920 did achieve was a complete split in the ranks of the socialists everywhere and the organization of the left-wing socialist groups into a new international movement of revolutionary Communist parties under tight Russian control.

Challenged by civil war and excited by the hope of international revolution, the Russian Communists yielded to the emotions of utopian fervor and fanaticism. The years from 1918 to 1921 were the truly extreme phase of the Russian Revolution. Along with the terror and one-party dictatorship, the Communists espoused the program of War Communism—an attempt by force and bureaucratic centralization to transform Russian society overnight into the communist ideal.

The new line was signaled in June 1918 by a series of sweeping decrees nationalizing all private business and industry. Foreign as well as Russian investors were expropriated without compensation, and this fact, together with the repudiation of tsarist and Provisional Government bonds, widened the gulf between Soviet Russia and the Allied governments. Administration of nationalized industry was divided between the *glavki* (head offices) in Moscow and local *collegia* representing the trade unions and the local Communists, in the manner of the ultrademocratic revolutionary ideal. This practice gave way gradually to the appointment of responsible individual managers, and by 1921 the principle of one-man authority in a bureaucratic hierarchy had become a permanent characteristic of the Soviet system.

Apart from keeping the Red Army supplied, the economic performance of War Communism was dismal. The railroads broke down and large-scale industry ground to a virtual halt. The government financed itself through the printing press and caused a runaway inflation, but welcomed this as the "withering away" of money. Attempts were made to supplant unequal money wages with equal rations in kind, but the equality of War Communism was an equality of impoverishment that left little incentive for individual effort. Lenin recognized this problem and shocked the party idealists by insisting on a shift back to graded salaries and piece-rate wages, which remain to this day standard practices of the Soviet regime.

The worst feature of all under War Communism was the forcible requisitioning of food from the peasants. This practice became necessary to feed the army and the cities when the production of goods for sale to the peasants broke down and money became worthless. Requisitioning alienated the loyalty of the peasants, who would otherwise have been pushed into the arms of the Communists by the Whites' intention to restore land to the former landlords. Peasant resistance brought the Soviet regime to the verge of collapse in 1921 and compelled Lenin to reverse his economic policies drastically in order to stay in power.

In the spring of 1919 the Communist government of Russia experienced perhaps its most severe test. The White forces were reinvigorated by British and French support that was now avowedly antirevolutionary, and they converged toward Moscow from all directions. In Siberia, the tsarist Admiral Kolchak carried out his own coup, overthrew the SR's of the Constituent Assembly, and set up a military dictatorship. His forces then drove on Moscow from the east. General Yudenich attacked Petrograd from his base in Estonia. General Denikin (the successor to Kornilov when the latter was killed) moved north from the Black Sea coast. The Communists in central Russia desperately mobilized their resources, using the Communist Party organization as a means to control and command the populace. Their geographical position enabled them to strike back at the White forces one at a time, and Kolchak, Yudenich, and Denikin were defeated in turn in the spring, summer, and fall of 1919. This ended the serious White threat, though White forces under Baron Wrangel held out on the Black Sea coast until late 1920.

With their victory against the Whites and the Allied intervention, the Communists recovered much of the territory lost at Brest-Litovsk. In reoccupying national minority regions they used the device of formally independent soviet republics proclaimed by the local Communists when the Red Army moved in. In this manner the soviet republics of the Ukraine, Byelorussia, Azerbaijan, Armenia, and Georgia were set up between 1919 and 1921. At first they were legally linked to the Russian Republic only by treaty, though the Russian Communist Party controlled the local Communist leaders directly. The reality of union was formalized in 1922 with the creation of the Union of Soviet Socialist Republics embracing all six soviet governments. Meanwhile, Soviet forces gradually reoccupied Siberia and negotiated the withdrawal of the last of the Japanese in 1922. In the same year Communist control was established in Outer

Mongolia, restoring the satellite status that tsarist Russia had imposed on that former tributary of the Chinese Empire.

On its western border the Soviet government did not score such a successful recovery. Here the problem was the newly independent republic of Poland. Poland's eastern border with Soviet Russia was undefined, though the British Foreign Secretary Lord Curzon had proposed the Curzon Line following the approximate language boundary between Polish to the west and Ukrainian and Byelorussian to the east. The Curzon Line would have left a considerable Polish minority in the cities east of the border and fell far short of the ambition of the Polish government to restore the eighteenth-century, prepartition boundary. In the spring of 1920 the Poles attacked, and captured Kiev. Soviet Russia, staggering from the Civil War, threw what forces it could into a counterattack. The Poles collapsed, and the Russians shortly found themselves at the gates of Warsaw. They responded to the occasion by announcing the military expansion of the Revolution and supported a Polish Communist group in preparation for a take-over. This spur-of-the-moment venture was the only acknowledged use of the Red Army to spread revolution. The gambit was soon forgotten when the Poles, stiffened by French officers and supplies, counterattacked in their turn and sent the Russians into full retreat.

Hostilities with Poland were ended by the Treaty of Riga early in 1921, which restored the old provisional boundary—about 150 miles east of the Curzon Line. This left several million Ukrainians and Byelorussians under Polish rule. One of the most pressing objectives of Stalin's foreign policy in the period of World War II was to annex this *irredenta* to the Soviet Union.

Other *irredenta* were created when the three Baltic states of Estonia, Latvia, and Lithuania successfully declared and maintained their independence with British support, and when Rumania took advantage of the Civil War in Russia to annex the largely Rumanian-speaking province of Bessarabia in the southwest. All these areas were targets of Stalin's restorationist ambition when World War II began.

The close of the Civil War and the peace with Poland did not ameliorate the atmosphere of crisis inside Soviet Russia. If anything, the lessening of external pressure encouraged the freer expression of opposition to the policies of War Communism, both inside and outside the Communist Party. Violence and privation brought workers and peasants in many parts of the country to the point of open strikes and uprisings against the government. Within the Communist Party the strength of the left-wing idealists, who had been sniping at Lenin's resort to bureaucratic authority ever since the Brest-Litovsk controversy, increased greatly in the fall of 1920. Their attitude of disappointment was exemplified by Alexandra Kollontai, leader of a group called the Workers' Opposition, when she declared: "The working class, as a class . . . becomes an ever less important factor in the affairs of the Soviet Republic. . . . Rejection of a principle—the principle of collective management in the control of industry—was . . . an act of deviation from that class policy which we so zealously cultivated and defended during the first phase of the Revolution."

In March 1921 the crisis came to a head when the sailors at the Kronstadt naval base, a stronghold of the Revolution in 1917, rebelled against the Soviet authorities and proclaimed a "third revolution" of the "toilers" against the "commissarocracy." The revolt was bloodily put down, but Lenin saw the handwriting on the wall and got the Tenth Communist Party Congress then in session to endorse some crucial policy changes. He called a halt to War Communism, suspended requisitioning from the peasants, and proclaimed a strategic retreat to what came to be known as the New Economic Policy or NEP. The NEP was a much more moderate and realistic approach to economic change, with toleration for individual peasant farming, small private business, and a normal money system. The state kept control of the "commanding heights" of transportation, utilities, and large-scale industry but decentralized their operation by placing more responsibility and ordinary financial accountability in the hands of managers. Lenin called the resulting system state capitalism, and it did in many ways resemble the organization of capitalist enterprise, apart from the fact that it was owned by the state.

These concessions made by Lenin in the interest of economic recovery and political survival brought the revolutionary era of Soviet history to an end. In effect, Lenin himself had carried out the Thermidorean Reaction of the Russian Revolution. The country was allowed a letdown in revolutionary strife and emotion and a return to the more normal concerns of life, even though the party of the erstwhile revolutionary extremists held firmly to its exclusive political power.

Within the Communist Party Lenin had to curb the disappointed adherents of revolutionary extremism and utopianism. By getting the Tenth Party Congress to condemn the left-wing utopians as a "petty-bourgeois anarchist deviation" and to ban any further activity by organized factions within the Party, Lenin undermined the possible growth of a multifaction system that might have permitted some freedom in Soviet politics.

The other main body of opposition to Lenin was the Trotskyists, who still hoped that a tough centralized dictatorship could push the Revolution ahead. Lenin removed the Trotskyists who had been in control of the Party's organizational machinery and replaced them with new men—Vyacheslav Molotov was one—who would do his bidding. The man who now became most influential in organizational work was Joseph Stalin. Stalin's eminence was confirmed in April 1922, when he was officially appointed to the new post of General Secretary of the Communist Party. These were the men and the machinery that would lead Russia into the phase of postrevolutionary dictatorship.

The first years of Communist rule, 1917 to 1921, had a profound effect on the future of Soviet Russia—more perhaps than the October Revolution itself. Politically, the Communists emerged from War Communism with a steeled and disciplined single-party dictatorship, a system which had not been a part of their original plan but which was implied in Lenin's political methods. As a result of the stress of civil war and the challenge of opposition inside as well as outside the Party, the Soviet regime had become a police state acknowledging no rights of individual political opinion or opposition. Instead of a dictatorship of the proletariat, it was a dictatorship by the Party over the proletariat and everybody else. Within the Party a dictatorship by the organization over the membership was fast developing. In the basic structure of power, the present totalitarian character of the Soviet system was already apparent.

In economic matters certain fundamental steps had already been taken to set revolutionary utopianism aside and recognize the bureaucratic and monetary necessities of modern industrial life. Similarly in foreign policy, the thrust of utopianism had stopped. The Soviet government was able to consolidate behind the doctrine of the Russian citadel, concentrate on getting control of a fraction of the socialist movement abroad, and prepare for whatever exigencies or opportunities the future might contain.

In one decisive way the Russian Revolution deviated from the pattern of the English and French revolutions. Unlike their counterparts elsewhere, the revolutionary extremists in Russia avoided being overthrown and stayed in power by changing their policies to follow the ebb in the revolutionary tide. This created a vast and growing discrepancy between Communist theory and practice—between what they did and what they were compelled to think about what they did. Soon the Communist leaders, particularly Stalin, created a unique practice of official falsification to make Marxist-Leninist theory appear to square with Soviet reality. Consequently, no one in Russia, not even the leaders, were free to see and understand the subsequent development of the country.

FOUR

THE EVOLUTION OF THE SOVIET SYSTEM

It is easy to regard Soviet Russia since 1921 as a state permanently fixed in all its essentials. The continuities in the Soviet system are obvious—dictatorship, the political monopoly of the Communist Party, the official philosophy of Marxism-Leninism, the methods of the totalitarian police state. This continuity is emphasized by the Communist Party itself. The successive rulers of the USSR— Lenin, followed by Stalin, and then Khrushchev—have all claimed that they are carrying out the basic program of proletarian revolution.

For a more realistic understanding of Soviet Russia, it is not enough to accept the surface appearance of continuity. It is necessary to think historically about the Soviet system. Thinking historically means two things above all: the recognition that change is always going on, and the realization that this change rarely conforms to the plans and intentions of people. Both of these propositions apply to Soviet Russia and need to be underscored because they are so often forgotten in talk about the Communist system. This is the fault of the Communist regime itself, because it represents itself as a society deliberately built according to the predictions of Marx and the plans of Lenin. Critics and defenders alike too often accept this premise and blind themselves to the evolution of Soviet Russia as an historical entity.

There are a number of sharply distinct periods in the history of Soviet Russia. These periods are more than stages in the progress toward a previously defined goal, as the Communist line has always claimed. They constitute a sequence of widely different *directions* of policy and effort. The New Economic Policy, followed by the Stalin Revolution and the subsequent shifts and consolidation, not to mention the Khrushchev succession of the 1950s, all represent profound adjustments to the realities of Russian circumstances and the continuing changes in Russia's world environment. Throughout, the Communists' theoretical plan of Marxism-Leninism has offered very little real guidance.

The continuities in the history of Russia since the Revolution rest on the given qualities of the Russian geography and people. Politically, the constants we observe have been preserved or revived out of the tsarist legacy. Russia was always and is now a highly centralized and essentially autocratic state where the political power is the dominant force in society and the individual is at the mercy of the government. Marxism-Leninism, as the officially enforced faith, has given the Soviet regime a continuity in appearance, in its propaganda, and in its political vocabulary. But this has masked a vast transformation in the policies and purposes of the Soviet system with respect not only to its own society, but, as we shall see in the next chapter, toward the outside world as well.

The New Economic Policy and the Succession Struggle

Lenin's New Economic Policy of 1921, devised to escape from the impasse of War Communism, set the character of the first long period of postrevolutionary Communist rule, up to 1929. During this time of the NEP Communism adjusted itself broadly to the realities of Russian life and the limitations of human nature. Lacking the internal industrial maturity or the external support of world revolution, Lenin made the retention of power his basic concern and reverted to the kind of approach he had sketched out in the 1900s: dictatorship by the party of the proletariat while Russia completed its bourgeois revolution and built up the industrial base for socialism. "Building socialism" was the Communist slogan right up to Khrushchev's time, much as it might confound the Marxian supposition that change in the political superstructure depended on prior development in the economic base.

Economically, the NEP was a quick success. Agriculture, based on individual peasant farming and a free market, recovered rapidly, though not soon enough to forestall the deadly famine of 1921-1922 in the Volga basin. With the simultaneous demise of the commune and the landholding class, the Russian peasantry was more individualist than at any time before or since. Nevertheless—or rather, for this reason—the amount of marketed food surplus available for the cities and for export never reached prewar levels, because the poor peasants preferred to consume most of what they grew on their newly enlarged holdings. Most of the surplus came from the minority of prosperous farmers, the kulaks, who were encouraged by the Communist government until the rude end of the NEP in 1929.

Soviet industry recovered from the low point of War Communism more slowly. Only by 1926 or 1927 was the prewar industrial plant brought up to full capacity, an achievement which then confronted the Soviet government with the problem of how to plan and finance the further expansion of industry. The organization of industry itself was decentralized, with much responsibility in the hands of the directors of state-owned enterprises and trusts. State-owned firms did business with one another and with private businesses under normal market conditions and recognized legal contracts. Most retail trade and small-scale manufacturing was denationalized and turned over to a new class of enterprising though unsavory businessmen known as the Nepmen. Wage equality was still held up as the ideal, but inequality based on skill, effort, and responsibility became the practice. The trade unions were excluded from any meaningful role in the control of industry, but under the leadership of Michael Tomsky they did have considerable power to negotiate for the workers' rights and living conditions.

In government, the NEP witnessed the return of all the old bureaucratic patterns and habits that the Revolution had hoped to destroy. Left-wing efforts to defend democracy in the army, industry, and the soviets collapsed during War Communism, and after the Tenth Congress in 1921 democratic forms within the Communist Party rapidly became a mere façade. Lenin warned frankly of the bureaucratic problem in 1923 (after the onset of his last illness): "Our machinery of state is very largely a survival of the past. . . . It has only been slightly touched upon the surface, but in all other respects it is a most typical relic of the old state machine."

The bureaucratic organization of the Communist Party was perfected between 1921 and 1923, owing largely to the work of Stalin. The nominally democratic local and regional organizations of the Party came under the domination of their respective secretaries. During the Civil War the central leadership began the practice of "recommending" secretaries, who were full-time, paid executives, to the local organizations. This practice continued and increased, and the secretaries were transferred from place to place to suit the convenience of the central authorities. In this manner the full-time Party officials became a distinct group, separate from the ordinary Party members and effectively dominating them. When Stalin got control of the Secretariat he used it to build a political machine of secretaries in the Party loyal to him. By 1923 he could control the election of a majority of the local delegates to the Party Congress and thus pack the Central Committee with his own supporters. In effect, Stalin controlled the body to which, as General Secretary, he was nominally responsible. It was only a matter of time and opportunity until he could remove all his rivals from the Party leadership and make himself the unchallenged boss of the Party and the country. Personal power achieved through the Party organization has ever since been the core of the Soviet dictatorship.

As long as Lenin lived, the Party and the country enjoyed a sort of collective leadership, not only in form but even to some extent in practice. Though Lenin was governmental head as Chairman of the Council of People's Commissars, there was no official chief of the Party above the Politburo. (In 1922 this body consisted of Lenin, Trotsky, Zinoviev, Kamenev, Stalin, Alexei Rykov, and Tomsky, with Bukharin, Molotov, and Mikhail Kalinin, the Chief of State, as candidate members.) Lenin did not behave as an absolute dictator within the Party. Genuine debate and voting continued in the Party's top organs until the succession problem raised the political stakes too high for Lenin's heirs to proceed in this fashion.

The question of who would inherit Lenin's power was opened when Lenin suffered a cerebral stroke in May 1922, barely four and a half years after he had taken power. His natural successor was Trotsky, still clearly the number two man in the hierarchy, though he had frequently been at odds with Lenin. But since everyone still hoped for Lenin's return to health, Trotsky was reluctant to make any overt move to take over. On the other hand, the rest of the leadership resented Trotsky as a relative newcomer to the Bolshevik ranks and feared that his drive, brilliance, and military influence would enable him to take over as a new "Bonapartist" dictator on the model of Napoleon I in France. With the backing of the Politburo an informal *troika* or triumvirate of Zinoviev, Kamenev, and Stalin assumed leadership of the Party and the country.

In the fall of 1922 Lenin was sufficiently recovered to resume work and found much to criticize in the activity of his lieutenants. He voiced misgivings about the revival of bureaucratic practices and was particularly disturbed by the trend toward Russian domination over the non-Russian national minorities, which he blamed on the "Great-Russian chauvinism of russified non-Russians," above all on Stalin. In December 1922 and January 1923 Lenin dictated the notes on his potential successors which have come to be known as his Testament. He warned of a potential rivalry between Stalin and Trotsky, "the two most able members of the Central Committee," and observed: "Comrade Stalin, having become General Secretary, has concentrated an enormous power in his hand; and I am not sure that he always knows how to use that power with sufficient caution." A week later, in a postscript, Lenin made up his mind:

> Stalin is too rude, and this fault, entirely supportable in relations among us Communists, becomes insupportable in the office of General Secretary. Therefore I propose to the comrades to find a way to remove Stalin from that position and appoint to it another man who in all respects differs from Stalin only in superiority. . . .

Fortunately for Stalin, the Testament remained unknown until he had enough power to deflect its impact.

To deal with the problem of Stalin, Lenin invited Trotsky to take action. At this point Lenin was felled by a final stroke that left him half paralyzed, and Trotsky failed to move, apparently calculating that he might better work with Stalin against his older rival Zinoviev. Stalin proceeded to cement his control over the Party organization through the Secretariat, and by the time Trotsky decided to move in the fall of 1923, it was too late.

The controversy in the Communist Party in late 1923 was fundamental, brief, and decisive. A coalition of the Trotskyists and Democratic Centralists defeated by Lenin in 1921, speaking in the name of Lenin's program, prepared a blistering though unpublished indictment of the Politburo majority for mismanaging the economy, neglecting the welfare of the working class, tolerating the return of bureaucracy, and violating democratic rules within the Communist Party. By December the controversy had broken out into the open in the newspapers and Party organizations, but at this crucial point Trotsky took ill and failed to give the opposition the leadership it needed. Stalin's machine easily overcame the opposition, and in January 1924, a week before Lenin finally died, the opposition was officially condemned as a "petty-bourgeois deviation" that violated the no-faction rule of 1921 and threatened to weaken the dictatorship of the proletariat.

The death of Lenin, though not unexpected, left his successors acutely anxious to maintain Communist Party unity and suppress opposition criticism. Collective leadership was officially in force, though Zinoviev was allowed to assume the number one position at the Party congresses in 1923 and 1924. Lenin's seat in the Politburo was given to Bukharin. His governmental post as Chairman of the Council of People's Commissars went to Rykov, perhaps the most cautious and colorless member of the Politburo. This signaled a distinct subordination of the government to the Party, a relationship that continued until after Stalin's purges.

Late in 1924 Trotsky tried to resume the political offensive by blaming the Party leadership for the failure of international Communist revolution. Taking advantage of the discrepancy between Marxist theory and the Russian facts, the Trotskyists suggested that Zinoviev, Stalin, and Bukharin were taking the NEP too far and appeasing the peasants and the Nepmen at the expense of the workers. By implication, the leadership was accused of becoming unsocialist, a tendency which the Trotskyists held to be unavoidable as long as Russia did not get outside support from proletarian revolutions in the more advanced countries. The Trotskyists were not really more revolutionary than the leadership, but they were trying to prove the inability of the leadership to keep Russia on the road to socialism.

The leaders whom the Trotskyists attacked were extremely sensitive about their theoretical virtue. Since they were afraid to make their policies any bolder, all they could do was insist that theory dictated their cautious course in both domestic and foreign policy as the only correct one possible. The man with the most effective theoretical answers to Trotsky was Stalin, though he accomplished this through obvious falsification and casuistry.

Stalin argued that Russia could now work toward socialism without waiting for international revolution, a prospect that had never before been voiced by the Russian Marxists. He found one quotation from Lenin, written in 1915, suggesting that certain countries might achieve socialism before others. Lenin had been thinking at the time of the most industrially advanced countries, but Stalin took the statement out of context and used it as his authority for declaring that Russia could and would proceed to build "socialism in one country." He condemned Trotsky's contrary theory of "permanent revolution" as a "Menshevik heresy" that betrayed "lack of faith in the strength and capabilities of our Revolution."

This theoretical discussion of socialism in one country was not of any great consequence for Soviet foreign policy. Neither faction was prepared to launch revolution abroad. "Socialism in one country" was important as the first clear-cut instance of Stalin's revision of Marxist-Leninist doctrine to make it square with the requirements of practical politics. The revision of doctrine, announcing a new version of what the doctrine was supposed to have been all along, required the strictest control of all public talk about ideology in order to suppress the very obvious opportunities to criticize Stalin's doctrinal falsifications. Thus arose the comprehensive controls over all aspects of thought which soon developed—controls bearing most heavily on thought among Communists and about ideology. The cumulative effect of all this was to cut the Soviet regime loose from any firm doctrinal moorings. No image of the earlier meaning of doctrine could be preserved, so that the only actual meaning of doctrine was that given it by the dictator to justify his policies of the moment. Doctrine thus lost its power to serve as a long-range guide or fixed motive and became instead an instrument of propaganda. While the language of Marxist-Leninist theory has remained more or less the same, theory no longer determines action; since Stalin's rise to power it is action that has supplied the meaning of theory.

The power which Stalin displayed by the mid-1920s, in his theoretical innovations as well as in his organizational work, began to alarm some of his erstwhile associates. In the fall of 1925 Zinoviev and Kamenev broke openly with Stalin and tried to unseat him at the Party Congress in December of that year on grounds that he was underrating the proletariat both in Russia and in the West and threatening to create a personal dictatorship. Kamenev declared in so many words, "I have arrived at the conviction that Comrade Stalin cannot fulfill the role of unifier of the Bolshevik staff." Zinoviev and Kamenev had the backing of Zinoviev's Leningrad Party organization, but Stalin had a firm grip on the rest of the delegates and easily turned back the challenge. The Leningrad organization was purged; Kamenev was dropped from the Politburo, and Zinoviev was ousted as Chairman of the Communist International in favor of Bukharin. Stalin promoted three of his own men to full membership in the Politburo—Molotov, Kalinin, and Klementy Voroshilov.

The Trotskyists took no part in Zinoviev's and Kamenev's challenge to Stalin. In 1926, after both groups had lost all power in the Party organizations, they belatedly came together to form the United Opposition. For a year and a half the United Opposition campaigned vehemently to try to discredit the leadership of Stalin and Bukharin on the issues of the lag in Soviet industry, the failure to put the interests of the workers ahead of the peasants, the suppression of democratic discussion in the Party, and the alleged failure to capitalize on revolutionary situations abroad.

The most significant issue in these debates was the controversy over economic planning and development. The Trotskyist economist E. A. Preobrazhensky argued at length for an intensive effort by the government to build industry and thus strengthen the proletariat. Industrial construction would be financed by taxing the peasants rather than waiting for consumer demand. Bukharin was the chief spokesman for the Party leadership; he stressed the need to move gradually and keep the peasants satisfied lest the Soviet government risk being overthrown. There was no difference on the principle of planning, but vast differences as to what kind of plan was best. The issues developed by the Soviet economists at this time are still relevant to the economic development of backward countries. As we will see, Stalinist Communism resembles the Trotskyist approach in playing down the role of consumer satisfaction and seeking to spur industrial development by dictatorial force.

Trotsky and Zinoviev, after being removed from the Politburo and the Central Committee on charges of factionalism, were expelled from the Communist Party in 1927. Hundreds of their followers met with the same treatment by the Fifteenth Party Congress in December 1927, on the grounds that they threatened to split the Party. Faced with this pressure, the opposition split; the Zinoviev-Kamenev group recanted and were temporarily readmitted to the Party the following year. The Trotskyists were turned over to the secret police and exiled in tsarist fashion to various remote parts of the country.

Trotsky himself was sent to Alma Ata in Central Asia. A year later Stalin decided to get rid of him altogether and expelled him from the country. While his followers one by one gave up their opposition and went back to serve Stalin, Trotsky commenced a ten-year odyssey during which he tried to mobilize a new international movement of anti-Stalin revolutionaries. This became the Fourth International of Trotskyist parties, many of which still survive as radical splinter groups in numerous countries today. Trotsky, meanwhile, moved from Turkey to France and thence to Norway in search of a haven and finally settled down in Mexico, where he was assassinated by a Stalinist agent in 1940.

The destruction of the left-wing opposition gave Stalin an unchallengeable position in the Soviet Communist Party. After bringing more of his own men into the top rank of the leadership, he was at last in a position to move against the remaining men who had shared power with him since 1922: Bukharin, Rykov, and Tomsky. Stalin maneuvered with the utmost political shrewdness to force these men into a position of opposition where he could convict them of factionalism as he had the Trotskyists. To accomplish this he boldly borrowed the industrial and international ideas of the Trotskyists themselves, though he conceded them no credit, and began to push for faster industrial construction and the collectivization of the peasants. These were the ideas which the Bukharinists feared would endanger the very existence of the Communist dictatorship. Thus did Stalin provoke the formation of the Right Opposition, with whom he did battle behind the scenes in the Party organizations in the fall of 1928.

This time the opposition stronghold was the city of Moscow itself. Stalin nevertheless had a firm grip on the central Secretariat and on the Party apparatus throughout the rest of the country, and it was easy for him to defeat the Moscow opposition. By early 1929 the Right Opposition leaders were defenseless, and Stalin proceeded to humiliate them publicly and expel them from their responsible posts. Bukharin was removed from the Comintern and replaced by Molotov; Tomsky had to surrender the trade unions to Nikolai Shvernik; Rykov was ousted as Chairman of the Council of People's Commissars in 1930 and replaced by Molotov (the Comintern then being turned over to Dmitri Manuilsky). The Politburo and Central Committee were reorganized to assure their full subservience to Stalin, and the public glorification of Stalin as the supreme national leader began. With no official government post, Stalin had nonetheless wielded his power in the Party to achieve for himself a degree of personal power and control far beyond what Lenin had ever enjoyed or even desired. Meanwhile, the maneuvers in policy which Stalin had made in order to consolidate his power left him committed fanatically to one special course of action for Russia's future development. This was the origin of the Stalin Revolution and the new period of cataclysmic change which it brought to the Soviet Union.

The Stalin Revolution and Its Aftermath

The violent policy changes that Stalin initiated in 1929 wrought effects more profound, in many respects, than the Revolution of 1917. Stalin himself later described the period as a revolution from above. In the organization of industry, agriculture, and cultural life, and in the functioning of the Communist Party itself, the Stalin Revolution laid down the present foundations of the Soviet system. Violence and repression were stamped deep in the fabric of Soviet life. The country emerged from this era, on the eve of World War II, with untold millions of prisoners in the labor camps and most of its own Communist leadership dead at the hands of the secret police.

Stalin's most positive achievement was to initiate the five-year plans of industrial construction. Planning, of course, was already an accepted Communist doctrine, though Marx had said little about it because he had assumed that the industrial economy would be fully developed by capitalism before the proletariat took over. In 1920 the State Planning Commission (Gosplan) was established, and during the 1920s it set out to develop a science of economic planning. Ironically, Stalin found the scientific plans of Gosplan too cautious, and the plan he ordered into effect in the spring of 1929 was a set of target commands rather than a rational calculation of over-all achievement. For political effect the plan was made retroactive to the fall of 1928. At the end of 1932 Stalin proclaimed the First Five-Year Plan complete ahead of schedule: it had actually run only three years and eight months. The combined targets of the plan were well beyond the resources of the country, so that fulfillment of the plan by particular industries depended on the allocation of materials and funds. Such decisions always favored heavy industry; naturally, the plan of heavy industrial construction was fulfilled while small-scale and consumer goods industry fell far behind expectations. This deficiency was compounded by enormous waste of effort and materials because of Stalin's insistence on speed and quantity at all cost, and because funds were often allocated to unprofitable construction projects.

Despite all these defects the First Five-Year Plan started a steady and decisive growth in Russia's economic potential. Steel production, to take the key indicator, rose from four and a half million tons in 1928 to six million in 1932, and then surged ahead to eighteen million tons in 1937, at the close of the Second Five-Year Plan. The total value of Soviet industrial output is difficult to measure because of errors in Soviet statistical procedures at that time, but the most plausible computation of output shows the index rising from the base of 100 in 1928 to 172 in 1932 and 371 in 1937.*

Stalin's industrialization drive was accompanied by new measures of centralized economic control. Managers assumed even stronger authority and responsibility in their plants, but their freedom of action was limited by the new requirements of planning. Fulfillment brought them bonuses and promotions; underfulfillment meant demotion or even arrest on charges of sabotage. Even today the Soviet planning system puts severe pressure on plant managers and other local officials, who have often responded by falsifying records, stealing materials, or committing other illegal actions.

The living and working conditions of industrial labor deteriorated sharply when the five-year plans began. The trade unions, which had concentrated on protecting the workers during the NEP, were now deprived of their autonomy and given responsibility for increasing the level of productivity. Labor discipline was tightened, and the incentive wage system became standard. Propaganda campaigns to increase productivity culminated in the celebrated Stakhanovite

* Donald R. Hodgman, *Soviet Industrial Production* (Cambridge, Mass.: Harvard University Press, 1954), p. 89.

movement of 1935, named after a miner who performed prodigious feats of digging coal. Stalin dismissed the old ideal of equality as "a piece of reactionary bourgeois absurdity." Meanwhile, living standards for the average worker were depressed, because the government allowed prices to rise faster than wages and thus reduced real wages. City housing became extremely crowded—one room or less per family—because the building program fell far short of the need to accommodate the influx of peasants who came to work in the new industry.

Simultaneously with the First Five-Year Plan, the government determined to eliminate the areas of private enterprise that had been permitted during the NEP. The small-scale businesses of the Nepmen were all nationalized again, and most rural handicraft work was discouraged. The government has thus enjoyed a monopoly ever since in all forms of trade and industry, and this has permitted concentration on industrial and military expansion at the expense of consumer goods and services.

Stalin's drive for industrial construction had to have some source of financing that would channel the necessary labor and resources into capital investment. In Russia's development Stalin was playing the part that Marx, along with most of the classical economists, had ascribed to the private capitalists. However, Soviet socialism ruled out both native capitalists and foreign lenders as sources of capital. Stalin's only means of financing his drive for industrial construction was to resort to a system of forced saving and forced investment by the Soviet people themselves—the same approach that the Trotskyist economists had put forth during the 1920s. This was accomplished partly by underpaying the city workers and imposing a heavy turnover tax on their purchases. Another important source of capital was the exploitation of the peasants; this was the real economic purpose behind the new system of collective farms.

Collective agriculture, like economic planning, had been a vague but accepted Communist goal since the Revolution. The roots of the idea went far back in native Russian socialist thought of the nineteenth century. Some experimental farm communes had been set up during War Communism (some monasteries even tried to survive by declaring themselves communes), but during the 1920s Russian agriculture became overwhelmingly individualistic. The collective farms of the 1930s were not a continuation of the old peasant commune but a new institution, justified in terms of the Russian tradition and Marxist doctrine but intended to guarantee the delivery of the grain supply to the state.

It is not certain that collectivization was the only way or the best way to support the industrialization drive, but it is fairly clear that Stalin became committed to both for political reasons. He began to put pressure on the kulaks in 1928, and in 1929 he ordered the whole-sale collectivization of the Soviet peasantry. During the winter of 1929-1930 nearly half the peasants in the country were organized into collective farms, ostensibly by their own wishes. Kulaks were deliber-ately excluded from the farms, and then, because of their alleged resistance to collectivization, they were systematically dispossessed and deported. Literally millions of peasants—kulaks, suspected kulaks, or any who resisted—died in transit or languished in new "corrective labor camps" in Siberia. Violent peasant resistance frequently broke out, particularly in the Ukraine and the southeastern part of Euro-pean Russia. These were the regions which the government tried to collectivize first and fastest because they were the main areas of sur-plus food production, but they were also the areas where the peasants were staunchly individualistic by tradition.

Collectivization did not actually mean relocation of the peasants, most of whom already lived in compact villages. It meant the con-fiscation of land, tools, and animals and the organization of collective village work in which the villagers were supposed to share. The ad-vantage to the state lay in the direct taxes and fees for machinery that the collective farm had to pay and in the obligatory deliveries of specified quantities of produce that the farms had to supply at arti-ficially low prices. Many villagers protested the collectives by slaugh-tering and eating their livestock. Soviet animal husbandry did not recover to the precollectivization level until after the death of Stalin, while the *per capita* supply of meat has not yet reached the NEP standard.

By the spring of 1930 Stalin recognized some of the harm that was being done, blamed his subordinates for the difficulties, and allowed a retreat. Half of the new collective farms were broken up. Then col-lectivization was resumed more gradually, encompassing 50 per cent of the peasants by the end of 1931 and 90 per cent by 1936. Such damage had been done to farm capital and work routines, however, that the added impact of drought in 1932 caused the southern part of European Russia to suffer another devastating famine in the winter of 1932-1933. Deaths from hunger and malnutrition probably ranged into the millions; the figures are uncertain because the Soviet govern-ment never admitted the fact of the famine at all.

The effectiveness of collectivization as a system to guarantee cheap food for the government to sell expensively in the cities is demonstrated by the fact that the amount of grain collected by the government increased steadily right through the famine years even though the total grain crop fell disastrously. It was the peasants who had to bear the hardship. Thanks to the crisis of 1932-1933, however, the peasants did win a significant concession. Henceforth each peasant family was allowed to till its own private plot and market its produce freely—a limited return to the NEP compromise. Since then, most of the food for the peasants themselves and a large proportion of the vegetables and animal products for the cities has come from these plots.

The stresses that Russia experienced during the time of the First Five-Year Plan and the collectivization were so severe that political repercussions were felt even at the highest level of Stalin's political machine. Many Stalinists became alarmed, as the Bukharinists had been, that the inhuman rigors of Stalin's policy might cause the Soviet regime to be overthrown altogether. By the time of the famine a moderate faction had taken shape in the Politburo under the leadership of the Leningrad party secretary, Sergei Kirov. Kirov had risen rapidly in the hierarchy, and after 1930 he was regarded as Stalin's second-in-command. Stalin yielded temporarily to the Kirov group, accepted the private plot compromise in the collective farms, ended the food rationing that had been in effect since 1929, and agreed to a higher priority for consumers' goods in the Second Five-Year Plan set for 1933 to 1937.

The period of relaxation in 1933 and 1934 proved brief. In December 1934 Kirov was assassinated—with the complicity of the secret police and Stalin himself, it now appears. Nevertheless, Kirov's death was taken as the pretext for a sweeping roundup of suspected opponents of Stalin, and the four-year political convulsion of the Great Purge had begun.

The most spectacular side of the Great Purge was the liquidation of most of the old opposition leaders in the course of the famous Moscow Trials. In 1935 Zinoviev and Kamenev and some of their followers were tried as accomplices in the Kirov affair and sentenced to prison. In 1936 they were brought to trial again on the charge of plotting with Trotsky to overthrow Stalin and restore capitalism. All the accused confessed, probably in the hope of winning clemency, but they were shot anyway. The second batch of defendants were close supporters of Trotsky, including Karl Radek, Grigory Piatakov, and Grigory Sokolnikov. They confessed to plotting with Germany and Japan to partition the Soviet Union; most got the death penalty, and the others disappeared in prison. Finally, in 1938 the Right Opposition leaders Bukharin and Rykov were tried and convicted, along with Henrykh Yagoda, the man who had started the purges as Commissar of Internal Affairs from 1934 to 1936. Tomsky had meanwhile committed suicide. Yagoda and his alleged accomplices were accused of a bizarre series of medical murders whose victims had included the industrial planning chief Valerian Kuibyshev and the writer Maxim Gorky. Again, all the defendants were liquidated.

Paralleling the trial of the oppositionists was a series of special purges with secret trials. These were directed particularly at the army and the leaders of the national minorities. In 1937 the Chief of Staff Mikhail Tukhachevsky and most of the other top officers of the Red Army were tried for plotting with Germany to overthrow Stalin, and executed. The governments of the union republics—particularly Stalin's home state of Georgia—were decimated in the same manner.

By 1937 these particular purges had broadened into a massive dragnet operation directed by the new Commissar of Internal Affairs, Nikolai Yezhov. This was the *Yezhovshchina* or "Yezhov business," in which hundreds of thousands of government and Party officials were implicated by the false confessions of their colleagues, arrested, tortured until they in turn confessed, and then summarily executed or incarcerated in labor camps.

Most incredible of all was the spread of the purge into the apparatus of the Communist Party itself. Stalin, suspecting new opposition (which his terror may actually have provoked), cleaned out almost the entire corps of Stalinist officials below the Politburo itself —more than 50 of the 71 members of the Central Committee, and all but one or two of the regional party secretaries. Three members of the Politburo (the Georgian Sergei Ordzhonikidze and the Ukrainians Stanislav Kosior and Vlas Chubar) and four of its five candidate members fell. In every case this purge of the Stalinists was secret and unexplained. History was rewritten to denounce the part played by the old oppositionists, but the new victims were taken out of the history texts altogether. In the language of George Orwell, they became "unpersons."

The distinction among the various kinds of purge was underscored by the selective rehabilitation of the victims' memory under Khrushchev. Khrushchev condemned the purge of the army, the bureaucracy, and the Party apparatus as a crime stemming from the "cult of personality." (He sidestepped the question of his own role in the purges, as Moscow secretary to 1938 and then as party secretary for the Ukraine.) Khrushchev hinted that the old oppositionists did not deserve the death penalty, but he steadfastly held to Stalin's condemnation of them as anti-Leninist deviationists—this despite the clear evidence that the opposition detected the menace of Stalin ten years before the purges began.

One final step in Stalin's purges was the removal of the purgers themselves. Yezhov was relieved from the NKVD late in 1938 and shortly disappeared, along with a large number of his men who were blamed for "excesses." Control of the police was given to another Georgian, Lavrenty Beria. Stalin had now eradicated all sources of opposition, cowed his remaining subordinates, and divided the channels of power among the Party, the police, and the army, so that no group or institution could challenge his personal rule.

Just as the purges were getting under way Stalin took steps to make his regime look more respectable on paper. He had a new constitution for the USSR drawn up, and put it into effect in 1936. The principal change under this document was to eliminate the formal distinctiveness of the Soviets as a system of government, with their class representation and pyramid of indirect elections. The Congress of Soviets and the Central Executive Committee gave way to the present bicameral, directly elected Supreme Soviet. The local and regional soviets were also to be directly elected. Class restrictions on voting were theoretically abolished. Executive power remained formally vested in the Council of People's Commissars, with Molotov as Chairman. In its reorganization of the soviets the Stalin Constitution abandoned the political forms on which the Communists had originally based much of their claim to revolutionary virtue, but these forms had already lost their meaning with the transfer of power to the Communist Party hierarchy. The purges accompanying the Stalin Constitution merely underscored the emptiness of that document as a promise of democracy.

Apart from the new constitution, Stalin made a number of pronouncements during the 1930s that served to bring Communist theory more in line with his own totalitarian practice. Back in 1924 he had already gone beyond most of his associates in spelling out the role of the Communist Party to lead and discipline the working class, not only to carry out revolution, as Lenin had stressed, but also "to maintain the dictatorship, to consolidate and expand it in order to achieve the complete victory of socialism," an end requiring "iron discipline" and "complete and absolute unity of action." Stalin was forced to concede at this time that "when classes disappear and the dictatorship of the proletariat withers away, the Party will also wither away." His actual conduct in power belied any early expectation of such "withering." In 1934 Stalin addressed himself to just this question, ridiculed the thought that the state could be dismantled while the "class struggle" was still going on, and asserted:

> We must realize that the strength and prestige of our party, state, economic, and all other organizations, and of their leaders, have grown to an unprecedented degree. And precisely because their strength and prestige have grown to an unprecedented degree, it is their work that now determines everything, or nearly everything. There can be no justification for references to so-called objective conditions. . . . The part played by so-called objective conditions has been reduced to a minimum; whereas the part played by our organizations and their leaders has become decisive. . . .

Here Stalin showed that he could change the most basic propositions of Marxian historical materialism to make the doctrine appear to square with the realities of the totalitarian state.

Stalin even tried to make the Great Purge square with Marxism. In 1937 he advanced the notion that:

> The more we move forward, the more success we have, then the more wrathful become the remnants of the beaten exploiter classes, the more quickly they turn to sharper forms of struggle, the more mischief they do the Soviet state, the more they grasp at the most desperate means of struggle, as the last resort of the doomed. . . .

This position was too much for Stalin's successors, and in 1956 they rejected it along with their repudiation of the purges. But Stalinist Marxism, with its emphasis on the role of leaders, organizations, and ideas rather than impersonal economic trends, is still the foundation of official Soviet thinking. Soviet ideas and Soviet policies over a wide range of matters ceased to be governed by the original meaning of Communist doctrine and conformed instead to a new amalgam of old and new beliefs which Stalin promulgated in the name of Marx.

The Transformation of Soviet Thought and Society

In the history of Soviet intellectual life and social policy the novelty of Stalinism stands out in sharp contrast to the original direction of the Revolution. Stalin turned the Soviet state into a unique structure serving rapid development and national power and gearing the individual to these overriding governmental objectives.

The present norms of Soviet social and cultural life were laid down somewhat later than the foundations of the totalitarian order in politics and economics. In the realm of intellectual and social policies the Revolution lasted through a dozen years of innovation and liberation. This was followed during the time of the First Five-Year Plan by a transitional period when the machinery of totalitarian control over thought and social life was being erected. Finally, in the mid-1930s, came a series of policy changes and reversals under command from Stalin, with the net effect of a veritable counterrevolution in the intellectual requirements and social goals of the regime. The conservative line initiated by Stalin has been the basis of Soviet cultural standards and social legislation ever since.

The years of the Revolution and War Communism were a time of chaos in Russian society and of postponement in cultural creativity. Revolutionary experimentation in thought, the arts, education, and social norms flourished during the NEP, before the Communist Party contemplated imposing thought controls beyond the censorship of overtly anti-Communist political opinion. The entire period 1890-1930 can be regarded as one epoch in the history of Russian thought. The cultural activity of the 1920s was a continuation or resumption of trends that had commenced 20 or 30 years before—the movement of modernistic criticism and self-expression in the arts, literature, and philosophy, in which Russia had been in the vanguard.

The Bolsheviks, when they took power, did not represent the most advanced currents of Russian culture. They exemplified the older intellectual fashions of the Russian revolutionary movement, particularly its simplified philosophical materialism and its subordination of artistic values to political and social progress. Many Communists—particularly those of the working class who had no experience in the West—had a profound distrust of the new ideas.

While many Russian intellectuals fled the country during the Civil War, others sympathized with the Revolution and during the 1920s enjoyed a cultural climate in which they could resume the experimentalism of the early 1900s. Every conceivable variant of modernism or futurism was practiced in literature and the arts, each stylistic school claiming to represent the new "proletarian culture." In fact, the masses had little contact with the new art, for the country (particularly the peasants) still had to conquer illiteracy and gain an appreciation of the simplest classical culture.

Social thought in the 1920s displayed the same anomaly as the arts, in striving for the most advanced, liberating policies in a country whose masses were scarcely civilized. In the name of equality of the sexes the intellectuals were proclaiming free love and the "post card divorce," while the peasants were still treating their women as chattels. Communist educators endorsed progressive education with "learning-by-doing" and student democracy aimed at the eventual "withering away of the school," while in most of the country there was no adequate schooling of any sort. Law and criminology sought to absolve the individual of guilt and blame the social heritage. Philosophy and psychology explained man in purely biological and deterministic terms. In sum, the revolutionary vision of man in society reaffirmed the hope of the eighteenth-century Enlightenment—in Marxist language—that human nature was naturally good, that evil came from class exploitation and oppressive institutions, and that all forms of authority and coercion would steadily wither away as Russia approached the classless society of free and equal citizens.

These hopes of the 1920s would have been utopian anywhere, let alone in Russia with its colossal problems of economic and cultural development. They were nonetheless genuinely held by the leading lights in most specialized fields of thought, though perhaps less by the political leadership in the Communist Party. But these revolutionary hopes, like most of Russian thought since the westernization in the eighteenth century, did not have a foundation in Russian society as a whole. Cultural unity could be gained only by pulling the masses up or pulling the thinkers down. Stalin undertook to do both.

Between 1929 and 1932 Soviet intellectuals for the first time felt the full force of totalitarianism. In one field after another Stalin or his lieutenants intervened to impose their views of art or philosophy and give the nod to the Party faithful to enforce the ultra-Marxist line in each field. All art and literature had to be "proletarian" in a crudely propagandist way. All history had to be cast in the terms of economic determinism. Economics and political theory had to recognize the decisive role of the government and its leaders in building the industrial economy. "Party spirit"—i.e., abject justification of the dictator's preferences—became the standard in every field of thought. Objective respect for the truth was condemned by Stalin as "rotten liberalism." Nonconformists who tried to preserve old "bourgeois" views were purged, by censorship, unemployment, and imprisonment.

Between 1932 and 1936 it became clear that Stalin's imposition of ultra-Marxist requirements was ruining intellectual work altogether, without answering his propaganda requirements. Stalin's response was not to relax the controls but simply to use them in a different direction. He purged his own cultural watchdogs on charges of being anti-Marxist and installed new cultural leaders who would heed his preference for traditional ideas under Marxist labels.

The official organizations of writers and artists were purged between 1932 and 1934 and ordered to follow the line of Socialist Realism. Socialist Realism, "national in form and socialist in content," has been the official label for Soviet cultural policy ever since. In practice it means strictly classical forms, propagandist glorification of the leader, Party, and nation, and condemnation of all modernistic experimentation as "bourgeois formalism."

In the fields of social thought Stalin's conservative shift was particularly striking. He condemned as "vulgar economic materialism" the ultra-Marxist writing of history that had been imposed by Mikhail Pokrovsky, and sanctioned a highly nationalistic approach to Russia's past—with Marxist terminology. Earlier efforts to cultivate the culture of the non-Russian minorities were rejected as "bourgeois nationalism" and supplanted by a pronounced favoritism for the Great Russians as the model nation in the USSR. The theory of the withering away of the state was revised to postpone its effect indefinitely and allow for the unabashed perfection of the totalitarian state and a bureaucratic society.

In line with his reinterpretation of Communist Party theory Stalin heavily emphasized state authority and individual responsibility. Law, in both its theoretical and practical aspects, was rehabilitated as a permanent foundation of the Communist state. Criminology paralleled the purges by shifting the burden of guilt from corrupt society to rotten individual. The permissive attitude to relations between the sexes was repudiated as "bourgeois" and replaced by a rigid divorce code and a stifling public puritanism. Education was revamped to end the progressive approach of democratic self-expression and returned to the old disciplinary methods of authoritarian instruction and grading. For the sake of industrial productivity, labor relations were reorganized to stress individual responsibilities and material incentives.

In principle Stalinism made no excuse for social conditions or class status. The individual was to be promoted and rewarded insofar as he availed himself of training and strove to serve the state. All special privileges for the proletariat were abolished, and what were in fact social classes were recognized as the "strata" of workers, peasants, and "toiling intelligentsia." For the upper officialdom good pay, low taxes, rights to personal property, interest-bearing state bonds, and (after 1944) unrestricted inheritance became the rule to reward their efforts and loyalty.

One sphere of policy which did not evidence a clear shift was the area of religion. The Orthodox Church was persecuted periodically from the time of the Civil War, when it backed the Whites against Bolshevik secularism, up to the late 1930s. A notable shift by the Soviet government came in 1943, during World War II, when Stalin decided on an accommodation with the Church for its patriotic effect. The Church won *de facto* toleration and was allowed to revive the office of Patriarch in return for supporting the regime politically. For other faiths conditions became decidedly worse after the purges because of their association with minority nationalism.

In a broader sense Stalin's Russia did become religiously conservative, if we regard Marxist doctrine as a new sort of state religion. Like the state churches of bygone monarchies, Marxism was imposed on everyone in the Communist society, not just Party members, as an obligatory faith. Conformity of individual belief was presumed essential for the security of the state, and the revolutionary promise of free self-expression was quashed. Maintenance of the faith then required control of any area of thought in which the shifts and distortions of the regime might be called into question. The result is still with us: the propaganda state where all public thinking is as much couched in abstract doctrine as in any theocracy in history.

Stalinism Triumphant

The new society that Stalin fashioned in the name of Marx and Lenin was harsh but stable. It met its test of life or death in the crucible of World War II and survived, after near disaster and unprecedented human loss at the hands of the German invaders. When peace came Soviet Russia proved to have changed less politically and socially than any of the other belligerents, even though the physical and economic impact of the war was worse in Russia than anywhere outside Germany. Postwar Russia was still in spirit postpurge Russia, ruled by terror, shrouded from the outside world, guided by a crafty paranoid bent on the maximization of his power both at home and abroad. There was no relaxation until Stalin died in 1953.

In the Soviet leadership there was a surprising continuity from the late 1930s to 1953, in contrast to the political upheavals of the two preceding decades. Stalin, as General Secretary, had what was left of the Communist Party organization firmly in his grip, with the assistance of Georgi Malenkov as his Secretary for Personnel. Malenkov became a candidate member of the Politburo in 1941 and a full member in 1946. His chief rival as second-in-command and heir apparent to Stalin was Andrei Zhdanov, the Leningrad secretary, who advocated the aggressive expansion of international Communism and was responsible for a severe tightening of the controls over doctrinal discipline and cultural expression. Following Zhdanov's death in 1948 his followers in the Party hierarchy were purged in the so-called Leningrad Affair. Malenkov then moved up to the number two spot and seemed to have Stalin's blessing for the succession when the dictator died in 1953.

Among Stalin's other lieutenants was Vyacheslav Molotov, Chairman of the Council of People's Commissars from 1930 to 1941. In 1939 Molotov was given the additional post of the Foreign Commissariat, to replace Maxim Litvinov and prepare the pact with Germany. Stalin took over the Chairmanship of the Council of People's Commissars himself in 1941 shortly before the German attack, and he headed both the government and the Party until his death. Stalin's crony Voroshilov was Commissar of War until Stalin took the post himself after war broke out. After the war this office went to Nikolai Bulganin. The key post of Internal Affairs was held after 1938 by Lavrenty Beria, who achieved Politburo rank in 1946. Other full members of the Politburo were Lazar Kaganovich (industry), Anastas Mikoyan (trade), Andrei Andreev (agriculture), Mikhail Kalinin (titular Chief of State from 1919 until his death in 1946), and Nikita Khrushchev, First Secretary of the Communist Party of the Ukraine since 1938.

Stalin made it a point to keep his lieutenants and the institutions they operated isolated from one another. The top Party committees rarely met, and there was no Party Congress from 1939 to 1952. In 1949 Stalin weakened the Politburo members by relieving them of their ministries (as the commissariats were conservatively restyled in 1945) and splitting the ministries, including the police and the military, among some 40 or 50 lesser men. Finally, in 1952 the Politburo was diluted by expanding its membership from 11 to 25. Apparently, Stalin intended by these steps to make it easy for Malenkov to assume individual power when the time came.

The war, for all its rigors, caused little internal threat to the stability of Stalin's regime. He did relax the enforcement of Communist doctrinal discipline, and gained more than the equivalent in patriotic fervor. In the battle zone it was another matter. Soviet troops, badly deployed, their morale undermined by the experience of the purges, surrendered by the hundreds of thousands in the first months of the German attack. The civil population of occupied zones often welcomed the Germans as liberators, particularly in the Ukraine and the North Caucasus. Numerous Soviet prisoners of war volunteered for service with the Germans. General Andrei Vlasov, captured in 1942, was allowed to organize an Army of Liberation composed of some 50,000 anti-Stalin Russians, while over half a million Soviet nationals served under direct German command.

Had Germany used political warfare more effectively, there is little doubt that Stalin could have been defeated and overthrown in 1941 or 1942. This would have meant an overt restoration on the pattern of other social revolutions—a restoration certainly abolishing the collective farms and Communist doctrine but not, to judge by the opinion of Soviet refugees, the authoritarian state or socialized industry. Like the English and French restorations, this Russian alternative would have been a compromise incorporating some of the original revolution.

Such an eventuality was ruled out by German error. Hitler was so dedicated to the enslavement of the "inferior" Slavic peoples that he refused to make use of the political capital offered him by Russian surrenders and defections. Hundreds of thousands of Russian prisoners were systematically starved in the first winter of the war. Occupied Russia found that it had only exchanged native totalitarianism for foreign terror. Forced laborers were deported, and Jews and other condemned groups were hunted down and shot. Partisan groups controlled by Moscow began to wage guerrilla warfare behind the German lines and laid the basis for the restoration of Soviet authority in the German-occupied zones.

Soviet rule, for those to whom it returned and for the "displaced persons" who returned to it, was almost as severe as during the purges. Nazi collaborators or suspects were liquidated, and millions of people were sentenced to forced labor camps on charges of treason allegedly committed while they were under German control or imprisonment. The labor camp population, swelled also by captured Germans and deportees from the Soviet minorities, may have reached five to ten million or even more in the postwar years.

The rigors of the Soviet propaganda and intellectual controls of the 1930s were restored in 1946, as the gloomy clouds of the Cold War gathered. In literature and the arts Zhdanov took the lead to reimpose the familiar line of Socialist Realism, with its conservative forms, Marxist vocabulary, and violently nationalistic and anti-Western content. With the ascendancy of Malenkov after 1949 the non-Russian minorities and particularly the Jews bore the brunt of an aggressive Russian nationalism which proclaimed the tsarist conquest to have been a benefit for all of Russia's borderlands. As for the natural sciences, some of the basic theories of modern physics and biology—Einstein's relativity and Mendelian genetics, for example—were condemned as "bourgeois idealism." Stalin's Russia at the end of his career was a gray and frightened land of theory without meaning, where practical engineering, military and industrial, was almost the only avenue for the creative mind.

The one area of real accomplishment of Stalin's regime in the later years, as in the earlier, was the progress of heavy industry, though still at the expense of consumer goods and agriculture. On the eve of the war, midway in the Third Five-Year Plan, Soviet heavy industrial output had passed the British (in absolute but, of course, not *per capita* terms). The German invasion was economically catastrophic: half of Russia's prewar industry, including the Donets Basin and besieged Leningrad, was in the war zone. Some industrial equipment was evacuated to the east, and by cutting the civilian economy to the bone the Soviet government was able to meet the basic manpower and munitions requirements of the army. The contrast with tsarist mismanagement in World War I was impressive. Anglo-American aid was an important supplement to the Soviets, particularly in automotive equipment and aircraft.

From a low in 1942, the Soviet economy was already partially restored by the end of the war, with steel production reaching 12 million tons in 1945. The five-year plans of expansion were resumed with the Fourth of 1946-1950 and the Fifth of 1951-1955, both of which put a premium on heavy industry. Thanks to this effort industrial output rose at the impressive rate of nearly 20 per cent a year, and when Stalin died Russia had reached an annual steel production of 38 million tons. In those sectors of the economy which counted most in national military potential, Russia's industrial revolution was now virtually complete. The Soviet perfection of an atomic bomb in 1949 testified to this.

Living standards for the Soviet population improved only slowly during the postwar years. Most of the collective farm peasantry was dismally exploited and impoverished, with an average individual cash income of less than $100 per year. Famine struck again in 1946 and 1947. Further centralized control was the regime's only answer to the lack of progress in agriculture, but without incentives the peasantry failed to respond. Factory labor was kept under the near-military discipline of wartime, and workers were virtually conscripted into the State Labor Reserves. The bad prewar housing situation was now far worse because of wartime destruction and the continuing lag of construction. The prewar standard of living for the average Soviet citizen was not achieved again until the early 1950s, and the the NEP standard was not reached until the Khrushchev era.

In 1952 Stalin convoked the Nineteenth Party Congress, at which he marked Malenkov as his heir and tried to weaken the possibility of an opposition by enlarging the Politburo. (It was simultaneously renamed the Presidium, and the old Orgburo was abolished.) Then, in January 1953 came the bizarre announcement of a "Doctors' Plot," allegedly a plan to murder the whole Soviet leadership as part of a United States and Zionist conspiracy. Possibly a new general purge was in the offing. Such was the tense political atmosphere when Stalin's death by cerebral hemorrhage was announced on March 5, 1953.

The Succession and the Khrushchev Era

The death of Stalin signaled a new test of the regime he had constructed. It is a measure of the strength of the Stalinist system that in its fundamentals it survived a succession struggle and the personal repudiation of its own creator. With some amelioration it remains the basis of Soviet political, economic, social, and intellectual life today.

No sooner was Stalin dead than his lieutenants undid most of the arrangements he had made for the succession. To be sure, Malenkov became government head as Chairman of the Council of Ministers, but he was forced to surrender direction of the Communist Party organization to Khrushchev. Khrushchev was probably the man least threatening to the other top leaders, but his position as First Secretary corresponded exactly to that of Stalin in 1922, and he was quick to capitalize on it. Meanwhile, the Party Presidium was strengthened by being cut down to 10 men. Its members (apart from Malenkov, Khrushchev, and Voroshilov, the new Chief of State) again took direct control of the key ministries: Beria in the police, Molotov in foreign affairs, Bulganin in defense, Mikoyan in trade. Kaganovich (without portfolio) probably supervised transport. Two new men, industrial planners Maxim Saburov and Mikhail Pervukhin, rounded out the new Presidium.

"Collective leadership" was proclaimed as the watchword of the new regime. Steps were quickly taken to repudiate the "Doctors' Plot" charges and to pardon many of Stalin's political prisoners. It seems possible that Beria took the lead in this direction, but his control of the police still posed a threat to his colleagues. In June 1953 they removed him from office—by shooting him on the spot, according to some reports. Then they split the police powers up and put them under the firmer control of the Party.

Along with the curb on police terror the new leadership made substantial economic concessions to the population, with pay and pension raises for the workers and tax relief for the peasants. In intellectual life the "thaw" gradually opened some ground for artistic independence, and Marxist interference in natural science was largely abandoned. Even in foreign policy there were substantial moves toward more normal relations with the non-Communist world.

Between 1953 and 1956 Khrushchev rebuilt the Party Secretariat and secured his control over the regional Party organizations. Early in 1955 he moved against Malenkov on charges of mismanaging the economy and underrating heavy industry. Malenkov was compelled to resign as Chairman of the Council of Ministers in February 1955 and was relegated to the Ministry of Electric Power Stations. The premiership then went to Nikolai Bulganin, who was replaced as Minister of Defense by the World War II hero Marshal Georgi Zhukov. For the next two years the Soviet leadership appeared to be a diarchy of Khrushchev and Bulganin.

In February 1956 the first post-Stalin Party Congress, the Twentieth, was held. Khrushchev chose this as the occasion for a remarkable political gamble, his "secret speech" (actually read all over the country by the Party "agitators") attacking Stalin's "cult of personality" record of paranoid despotism since the purges. The Stalinist victims of the purges (though not the old oppositionists) were posthumously "rehabilitated"—readmitted to history in a favorable light. Khrushchev lamely skirted his own role and that of his associates in the purges by pleading that Stalin had kept them in ignorance. He went on to condemn Stalin's methods of terror and torture and to promise that they would never be resumed.

Khrushchev's motives in opening the case against Stalin are hard to assess, but he was probably trying to win popular favor and embarrass the senior Stalinists among his associates. Apart from the ironic outbreak of pro-Stalin riots in Soviet Georgia, the attack on Stalin was taken with quiet relief by the Soviet people. Its greatest political repercussions came in Soviet relations with Communist movements and governments abroad.

By the end of 1956 it appears that there was a movement afoot among the older Soviet leaders to unseat Khrushchev. Like the opposition of the 1920s against Stalin, the supporters of Malenkov and Molotov in the governmental hierarchy were stymied by Khrushchev's control of the Communist Party organization, which was now restored to the political pre-eminence it had enjoyed before Stalin's purges. Taking a leaf from Stalin's book, Khrushchev adopted a series of novel policies to provoke the opposition into an open fight: his virgin lands scheme of agricultural expansion, the radical decentralization of industrial administration, and overtures in foreign policy to such ostensible enemies as Tito's Yugoslavia, West Germany, and the United States. In June 1957 the opposition decided to strike. While Khrushchev was visiting Finland they convoked a meeting of the Presidium and voted to remove him from the post of First Secretary. He hurried back to summon the larger and theoretically more authoritative Central Committee and had it "democratically" override the Presidium. Khrushchev's victory was complete; not only did he stay in power, but he had Malenkov, Molotov, Kaganovich, and Saburov expelled from all their Party and governmental offices as an "anti-Party group." Marshal Zhukov supported Khrushchev decisively but showed too much strength; he was replaced as Defense Minister in the fall of 1957 by Marshal Rodion Malinovsky and consigned to obscurity. Finally, Khrushchev capped his victory by removing Bulganin as prime minister in 1958 and taking the post himself, thus acquiring all the formal power that Stalin had held. The individual succession had finally come to pass after all, though not with the man, manner, or policies intended by Stalin.

After 1957 the Soviet leadership became once again quite stable, despite hints that other neo-Stalinist conservatives may have been maneuvering against Khrushchev. Mikoyan remained as First Deputy Chairman of the Council of Ministers and elder statesman. Leonid Brezhnev and Frol Kozlov alternated as Khrushchev's chief deputy in the Party Secretariat, until Kozlov took ill in 1963 and Brezhnev moved clearly into the number two spot. Mikhail Suslov and Otto Kuusinen continued as the ideological leaders of the Secretariat and as members of the Presidium. In the lower ranks frequent transfers and replacements kept the Party hierarchy on their toes and ruled out any cohesive opposition to Khrushchev.

During the first five or six years after Stalin's death every current of change in the Soviet Union was for the better: steady industrial growth, improved living standards, more housing, less intellectual constriction, less international fear. Trouble began to appear in 1957 with Khrushchev's politically motivated interference in the top-heavy economic planning system, though Stalin's investment in technology paid off in that year with Russia's first successful launching of an artificial earth satellite or *sputnik*. By the fall of 1957 the Sixth Five-Year Plan was so badly disorganized that it had to be abandoned altogether; 1958 was the first peacetime year since 1928 that was not included in a long-term plan. Long-range planning was resumed with the Seven-Year Plan set to run from 1959 through 1965, but by this time the Soviet tempo of industrial growth had begun to decline appreciably. Khrushchev gave most of his attention to various experiments in the lagging field of agriculture but failed to correct the basic ills of overcentralized direction and insufficient peasant incentives. A crop failure in 1963 dragged the whole economy down to a net annual growth of about 3 per cent, and forced the Soviet government to make large foreign grain purchases for the first time in its history.

Grave disruption threatened to ensue from a radical educational reform proposed by Khrushchev in 1958. Just a year after the *sputnik* shocked American education into a new quest for quality, Khrushchev took Soviet education to task for its impractical overemphasis on academic subjects. He proposed to put all students of high school age to work in industry or on the farms, with schooling to continue on a part-time basis for the talented. Over the next few years Soviet educators redefined the reform to preserve educational continuity for most students, though with the inclusion of a large measure of the polytechnic training popular in the 1920s.

The post-Stalin thaw in cultural life proved to be limited in duration and scope. More rigorous controls were applied after the East European crisis of 1956, later eased up, then tightened again during the international crisis of 1962-1963. Yet certain truly basic changes in the attitude of the Soviet intelligentsia appear to have taken place since 1953: a restiveness, professional self-confidence, and passion for foreign contacts that the Party can defy only at a great price in morale and creativity. Writers ranging from the old Boris Pasternak to the young Yevgeni Yevtushenko tried to defy the regime's standards, while a true sign of change was the publication of Alexander Solzhenitsyn's fictional exposé of labor camp life under Stalin. Only in the realm of religion was Khrushchev harsher than Stalin: the Jewish faith was hounded with increasing cruelty, and even the Russian Orthodox Church encountered stiffer curbs on its propagation of the faith.

Khrushchev was 64 years old when he achieved supreme power in 1958, and he seemed content to make the most of the system he ruled without fundamental changes. In the new Communist Party Program laid down at the Twenty-Second Party Congress in 1961, he undertook to claim for his regime a historic place in the realization of Marxist theory by announcing that Soviet Russia had entered the final lap on the path to the Marxist utopia—the phase of "building communism." The class struggle was now over, he contended, and class differences had ceased to exist (though differential rewards for individual effort and responsibility are likely to continue indefinitely). Accordingly, Khrushchev announced that the dictatorship of the proletariat was at an end and that the Soviet state was now a "state of all the people." This notion was a patent distortion of Marxist fundamentals—as the Chinese Communists were soon to point out—but it suited Khrushchev's interest in self-righteous stability. He declared that the function of the state from this time on would be to complete the construction of the "material and technical basis of communism"—i.e., more industry and more education.

To comply with Marx's prediction that the state would wither away, Khrushchev called for the step-by-step transfer of governmental functions to "non-governmental public organizations." In fact, however, this means only that the totalitarian state would continue under a different label, since the Communist Party would continue permanently as one of these "public organizations," with its familiar power to control all other activities in Soviet society. During the early 1960s the Party assumed closer control of industry and agriculture, and the trend seems to be for the Party to become everything that the government used to be. It is less certain that this will always be accepted as the last word in Marxism.

Soviet Russia in the 1960s resembles a complex geological formation, whose successive layers date back to different periods in the past, with metamorphosis of the older strata under the pressure of newer accretions. The Soviet political system, and with it the most obvious official continuities, is the oldest element in Soviet society; its basic structure of one-party bureaucratic dictatorship was laid down in the revolutionary years from 1917 to 1921. The fundamentals of the Soviet economic system stem from the Stalin Revolution of 1929-1932, emphasizing planned industrialization, total nationalization and collectivization, and managerial discipline. Soviet social and cultural standards are still largely those of the Stalinist consolidation of the mid-1930s. The strands of doctrine are old, but they have been molded and twisted under the weight of hierarchical totalitarianism. The prevailing ideology of big organization and central control reflects the primary historical components of the Soviet structure —traditional tsarist centralism on the one hand, and modern Western industrialism on the other.

Does the future offer much prospect for evolution in the nature of the Soviet monolith? The historical viewpoint suggests two certainties: that some change will occur, but that the older historical traditions will persist. Russia will most certainly remain a centralized bureaucratic state, despite the likely increase in the restlessness of the intelligentsia. The progress of Soviet industry will not necessarily further democracy, contrary to the predictions of some authorities

FIVE

SOVIET RUSSIA AND THE WORLD

The history of Soviet Russia in world affairs is as complicated as the country's internal development since the Revolution.
Soviet Russia has not only been a major world power, but also the
heart of an international revolutionary movement of an almost religious character. Changes both in the international environment
and in the motives of the Soviet regime itself have repeatedly led
to shifts in the tactics of Soviet foreign policy and occasionally in
its general direction as well. A basic change also occurred in Russia's
relationship to the international Communist movement, as ideological sympathy was supplemented by controls to keep the movement
in the service of Soviet power interests.

Throughout the history of Soviet foreign policy there has been a
pronounced conflict between the theory and emotion of Marxist
revolution and the practical requirements of Soviet national security.
From each period of Soviet policy to the next one can see this
alternation of emphasis: revolution from 1917 to 1921; security to
1928; revolution to 1934; security from 1934 to 1945; revolution
thereafter, though revolution increasingly identified with the interests of the Soviet state. Finally, as we approach the present, it
appears that Soviet Russia is losing control of the revolutionary movement. Such may be the result of the conflict between the Soviet
leaders and foreign Communists—primarily the Chinese—who as-
pire to their own revolutionary future.

Soviet Russia in Isolation

The Revolution in Russia began with the fervent hope of world-
wide revolution. Indeed, the sense of mission to start the world
revolution was a prime justification for the Bolshevik seizure of
power. When the revolutionary period in Russia ended in 1921 the
hope of international upheaval was still unrealized. The Russian
Communists and their sympathizers abroad had failed to capitalize

on the chaos and unrest in Central Europe following World War I, except for abortive coups in Germany and Hungary. Capitalism, in Communist parlance, had achieved a new stabilization.

Under Lenin's pragmatic leadership the Soviet government adjusted to the postrevolutionary realities of the international situation. Soviet Russia was only one in a system of potentially hostile powers and badly needed trade and allies to improve its security. Foreign Commissar Georgi Chicherin, himself an ex-nobleman and tsarist diplomat, plunged unabashedly into conventional diplomacy and power politics, secured commercial agreements, concluded nonaggression pacts with Russia's neighbors, and sought recognition by the other great powers. A major diplomatic coup was the Treaty of Rapallo, an old-fashioned deal between Soviet Russia and the other lonely great power, Germany. By the mid-1920s most of the major and minor powers saw the necessity for establishing relations with Russia, swallowed their compunctions about defaulted debts and expropriations, and recognized the government of the USSR. The only important hold-out was the United States, which refused recognition until 1933.

Meanwhile, Soviet Russia still possessed, in the Communist International, the organization of foreign radicals who had rallied to the banner of world proletarian revolution after 1917. With the passing of the prospects for world revolution, the Soviet leaders had to make the Comintern serve the interest of Soviet security and survival while capitalism remained stabilized. The Russians therefore had to discipline the foreign Communists to work peaceably in a "united front" with anyone who would listen rather than attempt any actual revolutionary adventures, at least for the immediate future. The last Communist revolutionary effort was the abortive uprising in Germany at the time of the great inflation in 1923. After this the foreign Communist parties were rapidly "Bolshevized" as the Russians pressured them to select compliant leaders and expel the revolutionary purists.

Two of the most ambitious applications of the united front policy were made in Great Britain and China. In Britain the Communists supported the non-Communist trade-union movement, only to see the alliance break down completely at the time of the British General Strike in 1926. In China the Communists were ordered to join the revolutionary nationalist movement of Chiang Kai-shek and encourage it in the direction of a Soviet alliance. This venture failed altogether when Chiang, having won power, broke with Russia and purged the Communists from his movement. Chinese Communism would have collapsed altogether had it not been for the guerrilla warfare begun among the peasants by Mao Tse-tung. The failures of the Comintern's united front policy were bitterly debated in Russia, as the Trotskyists pointed to them to embarrass the leadership of Stalin and Bukharin. At the same time, factions arose in the Communist parties abroad in sympathy with each faction inside Russia. Matters came to a head in 1928 when the supporters of Trotsky were condemned and expelled from all the foreign Communist parties.

On the heels of this purge of the left wing came Stalin's move against the Bukharinist right wing. Stalin made use of foreign as well as domestic policy maneuvers to embarrass his opponents. He claimed that the stabilization of capitalism was coming to an end and that a "third period" of revolutionary action by the Comintern was in order. The third period line involved more talk than action, but it gave Stalin the opportunity to purge Bukharinists everywhere who opposed such rashness. Most of the right-wing Communists quit or were expelled from their respective parties and went over to the democratic socialists, while the Trotskyists proceeded to form their own revolutionary parties in the Fourth International. By 1930 there were very few Communist parties that had not lost a majority of their original leaders through purge or schism. The new Communist leaders, everywhere but in China, owed their tenure to Stalin's favor and had no choice henceforth but to follow every turn of the Soviet line. From this time until after World War II it is indeed possible to speak of a monolithic international Communist movement.

Meanwhile, the world economic crisis of the Great Depression beginning in 1929 seemed to bear out Stalin's prediction of a new revolutionary upsurge. The Communist parties gained more popular support, usually at the expense of the moderate Left. Germany again seemed the focal point of revolution. As the forces of right and left extremism ground the Weimar Republic to pieces, Stalin's strategy was to attack the Social Democrats as "Social Fascists" and let the Nazis overthrow the Republic to pave the way for the Communists. The result was an easy victory for Hitler in 1933 and the destruction of the German Communist movement as well as the Republic.

Stalin responded to this debacle, as to his earlier China defeat in 1927 and subsequent failures as well, by continuing obstinately on the same course until the disaster was compounded. Flexible in his choice of long-run strategies and goals, he was tactically rigid in the short run. The initial Communist reaction to the New Deal in the United States, for example, was to condemn it as a form of fascism.

By 1934 the clear threats of Nazi Germany and militarist Japan made it impossible for Stalin to continue an openly revolutionary course. Russian national security required allies at any cost, and the Comintern had to help. The result was a turnabout in the style and rationale of Soviet foreign policy and a new deviousness in the use of foreign revolution as an instrument of Soviet policy.

Soviet Russia in Alliance

Between 1934 and 1945 Soviet Russia behaved like an old-fashioned great power as a matter of survival, dictated by the shape of world power alignments before and during World War II. Externally, Soviet Russia resorted to all the familiar devices of alliances and diplomatic maneuvers in patent disregard of ideological affinities or antipathies. Internally, the old emotions of Russian nationalism were systematically cultivated and made a permanent part of the ethos of Stalinist Communism. For the international Communist movement the new line meant a tortuous course of sham and inconsistency, with a resort to nonrevolutionary appearances that, ironically, strengthened the movement considerably.

Soviet diplomacy made the new turn abruptly in 1934 when Foreign Commissar Maxim Litvinov espoused the doctrine of collective security. The Soviet Union joined the League of Nations, which it had previously denounced as a capitalist conspiracy, just as Germany and Japan were quitting it. In 1935 Russia's rapprochement with the democratic West took tangible form through the conclusion of defensive military alliances with France and Czechoslovakia. This combination of politically disparate powers recalled the Franco-Russian alliance of the 1890s and reflected the same mutual fear of Germany. As in the earlier situation, Great Britain, though tied to France, refused to cooperate with Russia—this time until it was almost too late.

The entire program of the Communist International had to be revamped to justify the Soviet policy of alliances. This was accomplished at the seventh and last World Congress of the Comintern in 1935. Georgi Dimitrov, the Bulgarian who headed the Comintern from 1934 until its demise in 1943, proclaimed the new line of the Popular Front, according to which all Communist parties were to play down revolution and seek cooperation with other parties in an antifascist coalition. In their new guise of nationalism and reformism Communist parties made considerable gains on every continent.

They gained their first real foothold in Asia and their only period of appreciable influence in the United States.

The Popular Front line introduced a permanent change in the basis of the Communist appeal. The Marxist call for immediate proletarian revolution was almost completely abandoned. Since the mid-1930s Communist propaganda has taken up the causes of labor, agrarian protest, nationalism, peace, and antifascism. The movement became and has remained inherently deceitful, thus increasing the need for organizational discipline to make up for inconsistencies in its theoretical position.

The two great tests of the Popular Front were in France and Spain, where Communist support contributed to election victories of socialist-liberal coalitions in 1936. For two years France had a shaky Popular Front government under Leon Blum, a Socialist, until the moderates' distrust of the Left caused it to fall. In Spain the right-wing military under Francisco Franco rose up to overthrow the Communist-backed Republic in a civil war from 1936 to 1939. Russia's role in the Spanish Civil War was devious in the extreme; simultaneous efforts were made both to maximize Communist political influence and to curb attempts at social revolution that might frighten Russia's democratic allies. From this time on Stalin seems to have become deeply suspicious of foreign Communists whom he could not directly control. He withdrew support from the Spanish Republic in 1938, leaving it to collapse, and purged most of the Soviet representatives who had been involved in the venture. He also liquidated almost all of the foreign Communists who had taken sanctuary in the USSR in the 1930s.

Simultaneously with the Spanish debacle Russia's experiment with alliances broke down. The British and French, faced with the rising threat of Nazi Germany, tried to appease Hitler by agreeing at Munich in September 1938 to the partial dismemberment of Czechoslovakia. Russia, though it was an ally of France and Czechoslovakia, was not invited to the conference, nor was Czechoslovakia. Stalin interpreted the Munich agreement as a green light for Hitler to move eastward, so he commenced his own counterdiplomacy to come to terms with Germany. After March 1939, when Hitler absorbed the rest of Czechoslovakia in violation of the Munich agreement, the British and French stiffened in their attitude. They tried to negotiate an agreement with Russia to guarantee Poland, but the talks broke down in the summer of 1939 over the Polish refusal to give Soviet troops the right of passage. Stalin removed the pro-Western Litvinov from the foreign office and entrusted the job to Prime Minister Molotov. The Soviets judged that their immediate advantage lay in a deal with Hitler, and in August 1939 the Communist and Nazi dictators astounded the world by concluding a nonaggression pact.

The 1939 pact with Germany was a cynical maneuver in the tradition of classical diplomacy, a move that largely wrote off the cause of international Communism and the considerable loss of allegiance that lay in store for the foreign Communist parties as a result of Stalin's accommodation with his erstwhile Nazi enemies. The pact provided for the division of all of Eastern Europe into German and Soviet spheres of influence and for the complete partition of Poland after the planned German attack. In contrast to the defensive and cautious diplomacy which Soviet Russia had followed ever since the Revolution, the Soviet regime could now expand by force of arms with German assent, while the Western Allies could do nothing.

From the fall of 1939 to mid-1940 Russia moved forward everywhere on its western border to recoup the losses of 1914-1921 and to gain a zone of defense in case of war with Germany. Russia attacked Poland three weeks after the German invasion on September 1, 1939. Eastern Poland, with its mainly Byelorussian and Ukrainian population, was annexed to the USSR and divided between the Byelorussian and Ukrainian republics. Soon afterwards the three Baltic states of Lithuania, Latvia, and Estonia were forced to permit Soviet bases on their territory and were annexed the following year, with the aid of small local Communist parties and sham plebiscites. The three countries were incorporated into the USSR as new Soviet republics. The same status was accorded the province of Bessarabia, which Rumania was compelled to return to Russia in mid-1940. It became the Moldavian SSR.

In the case of Finland Russian expansion met with unexpected resistance. The Finns refused to grant the bases demanded by Moscow, and the Soviets attacked. Although Soviet troops were thrown back in the initial phase of this "Winter War" (December 1939 to March 1940), their numerical superiority finally threatened to overwhelm the Finns. In the peace agreement the USSR got the bases it had originally demanded, plus a substantial slice of territory north of Leningrad. It also got the determined enmity of the Finns, who joined the German attack in 1941 as the only democratic country on the Axis side. Soviet forces again forced Finland to come to terms in 1944 under a settlement similar to the agreement of 1940. Finland continued to be a rule-proving exception as the only country invaded by the Soviet army that escaped the fate of Communist dictatorship.

Russo-German relations deteriorated steadily between 1939 and

1941, particularly after Germany had overwhelmed France and turned to tighten its hold on the Balkans. By the end of 1940 Hitler, like Napoleon more than a century before, decided to finish off his Russian ally before trying to humble Great Britain. The German timetable was delayed by an anti-Nazi coup in Yugoslavia and the campaign to crush Yugoslavia and Greece in April and May 1941. Meanwhile, Stalin made every effort to placate the Germans with grain and oil deliveries and to avoid any sort of provocation. He ignored warnings from the British even when the German attack was imminent. The German offensive on June 22, 1941, caught the Red army deployed close to the frontier without a proper defense in depth and took the Russians completely by surprise. Such was the disastrous end of Stalin's German alliance, a diplomatic failure compounded meanwhile by the defeat of France, Russia's only ally on the continent of Europe. The German attack perforce threw Soviet Russia into an alliance with Great Britain, extended to include the United States in December 1941 (though Russia avoided a state of war with Japan until 1945). This purely circumstantial cooperation was then rationalized on both the Soviet and Anglo-American sides as a natural and enduring coalition of peace-loving peoples.

The first phase of the war with Germany went badly for Russia. German armored columns cut through Soviet forces stretched thin along the border and enveloped them by the hundreds of thousands. Russian morale, both civil and military, was at a low point, and the out-generaled Soviet troops surrendered by whole divisions. Stalin proclaimed a "Patriotic War" on the model of the 1812 defense against Napoleon and pulled out all the nationalistic stops in his propaganda. Nevertheless, the Red army was driven steadily back until, by December 1941, the Germans had occupied the entire Ukraine and were pounding at the gates of Leningrad and Moscow.

Winter and overconfidence stopped the Germans in 1941 as they had Napoleon in 1812. Soviet reserves, better equipped than the Germans for winter warfare, finally counterattacked and drove the Germans away from Moscow. In a second great drive in the summer of 1942, the Germans struck to the southeast, with the apparent objective of breaking through to the Middle East and linking up with their Japanese allies. By fall the Germans had occupied most of the North Caucasus and were locked in the most bitter and decisive battle of the war with the Russian army at Stalingrad on the Volga.

Against a new Russian counteroffensive in the winter the Germans were less fortunate. Their garrison in Stalingrad, ordered by Hitler to stand at all cost, was entirely cut off and surrendered in February

1943. This was the decisive moment of the war; the strategic initiative now passed to the Russians. Under the supreme command of Marshal Zhukov the Soviet army launched its greatest offensive in July 1943 and moved steadily forward on all fronts until Nazi Germany finally collapsed in the spring of 1945.

When the Soviet Army entered Poland and Rumania in the spring of 1944, the political future of Eastern Europe became an immediate question. Military control proved to be the key factor. The Soviet drive through Rumania forced the Germans to evacuate the Balkans altogether in the fall and winter of 1944. Russia then secured the capitulation of Germany's allies Rumania and Bulgaria and linked up with the Communist guerrillas in Yugoslavia. In Poland, as the Russians approached Warsaw, they were welcomed by an uprising of the non-Communist Polish underground directed by the government-in-exile in London. To eliminate this political competition, the Russians suspended their advance and allowed the Germans to crush Warsaw. When German resistance finally crumbled in April and May of 1945, Soviet forces took over Hungary and Czechoslovakia and moved into their previously arranged occupation zones in eastern Germany and Austria. This military occupation laid the basis for postwar Communist rule in Eastern Europe. In the same fashion, the Soviet military occupation of Manchuria and northern Korea during the last days of the war against Japan secured a major base for Chinese Communism and made possible a Communist satellite government in North Korea.

Formal cooperation among the Anglo-American-Soviet allies worked reasonably well up to the very end of the war, despite portents of serious friction. In February 1945, at Yalta in the Crimea, Roosevelt, Churchill, and Stalin agreed on basic postwar arrangements. The Soviets participated in the formation of the United Nations in the spring of 1945 and in the Potsdam Conference on the future of Germany in July. In August, as promised, the Soviet Union intervened in the Far East to help defeat Japan and end the Pacific War.

During the war the Soviet leadership ceased altogether to speak of international Communist revolution. Stalin discussed the political future of Russia's neighbors in the democratic and nationalistic terms of the Popular Front. In 1943 he officially dissolved the Communist International. This act did not, of course, end the existence of the individual Communist parties or the allegiance of their leaders to Moscow. Communists played a major role in underground and guerrilla resistance movements against the German occupation forces throughout Europe and against the Japanese in China and parts of

Southeast Asia. Yet Stalin distrusted the Communist guerrillas because they were outside his control and threatened to upset relations with his allies. The Yugoslav Communists set up their own government in 1943 with no Soviet encouragement. When the Greek Communists attempted to do the same after the German withdrawal in 1944, Stalin looked the other way while the British forcibly reinstalled the royal government-in-exile. In China Stalin discounted Communist strength and pressed for maximum Soviet imperialist concessions from the presumably stable Nationalist government. On the other hand, wherever the presence of Russian troops made Soviet control secure, Stalin sent in cadres of native Communists who had been refugees in Russia.

Poland was the scene of the most serious interallied discord in the last months of the war. Here Stalin insisted on the repossession of *irredenta* in eastern Poland and on the establishment of a Polish government friendly to the Soviet Union. The latter was, of course, unacceptable to the Polish government-in-exile in London, which had severed relations with Russia in 1943 over the Katyn Forest massacre of Polish prisoners. Stalin proceeded to establish his own provisional government of Polish Communists as soon as his army had occupied part of Poland, and at Yalta he got Western recognition of this government and the Curzon Line boundary in return for his promise of democratic elections throughout Eastern Europe. The elections that came were largely a sham, signaling a new era of power politics and East-West conflict.

Soviet cooperation with Britain and America from 1941 until the defeat of the Axis had sufficed to destroy the most serious threats to Russian security and ambition both in Europe and in the Far East. Directly or through the agency of foreign Communists, Russia was able to move into the power vacuum left by the collapse of Germany and Japan. Soviet Russia entered the postwar world with unprecedented strength in arms and allies—a superpower matched only by the United States of America.

Soviet Russia and the Blocs

The Soviet Union responded to the post-World War II situation with a succession of steps to cement Communist control over as large an area as possible. In occupied Eastern Europe, Soviet pressure delivered the local military and police forces into Communist hands. The Communists first worked through coalition governments in reformist Popular Front style while they gradually undermined the opposition parties and prepared for one-party rule. By 1947 Poland,

Rumania, Bulgaria, and Hungary were one-party Communist dictatorships, though the Soviet Union described them as "peoples' democracies," theoretically inferior to Soviet socialism. Democratic government in Czechoslovakia was ended abruptly in February 1948 by a Communist coup. Guerrilla victories had given Yugoslavia and Albania Communist dictatorships of the most militant sort right after the war. In Greece the Communists resumed their rebellion in 1946, with aid from the Communist governments to the north, but British and American aid to the government, plus Yugoslavia's defection from the Soviet camp in 1948, helped bring the civil war to an end in 1949. The final Soviet satellite to be established in Eastern Europe was East Germany, where, after the breakdown of all cooperation between the Russians and the Western occupation forces, the Soviet occupation zone was officially constituted as the German Democratic Republic.

A new organization to propagate international Communism was the Communist Information Bureau or Cominform, set up in 1947 under the supervision of Andrei Zhdanov to link Russia, the satellite Communists, and the French and Italian Communist parties in opposition to the efforts of the United States to restore European prosperity. The Cominform itself did not accomplish anything particularly significant, but from 1947 to 1949 the Communist movement as a whole took its cue from Moscow and stood in revolutionary opposition to all democratic or colonial governments.

At the same time, Communist ranks were tightened in Eastern Europe. Tito of Yugoslavia, up to 1948 the most radical and faithful follower of Stalin, resisted Stalin's attempts to impose direct control through Soviet agents. In consequence, Yugoslavia was expelled from the Cominform in June 1948 and denounced as a traitor to the Communist movement. Tito and his aides mapped out their own model of the Communist ideal, somewhat less totalitarian than the Russian model, and successfully asserted their political and diplomatic independence. Albania, frightened by Yugoslav ambitions, drew closer to Moscow and purged its own pro-Tito faction. Many of the other East European Communists, disturbed by Stalin's political and economic demands, would have preferred to follow Tito, but this sentiment was nipped in the bud by a series of purges against the "national Communists" in the other satellites. From 1949 to 1953 most of Eastern Europe was locked in the grip of complete Soviet domination, exploitation, cultural russification, and police terror.

After 1946 the most serious Soviet-Western friction took place in Germany. In accordance with the Yalta and Potsdam agreements,

Germany had been divided into four occupation zones (American, British, French, and Soviet, and a "Polish administration" east of the Oder-Neisse line), but the country was supposed to be administered as a unit and democratized in preparation for a peace treaty and the restoration of a national government. Conflict quickly arose because of the Western desire to secure a prosperous and stable Germany and the Soviet determination to exact maximum reparations and keep Germany enfeebled. Conflicting policies in the Western and Soviet zones led to the severance of economic and financial relations between the two sectors. In mid-1948 the Russians blockaded all ground communication to West Berlin, which was administratively and economically part of West Germany, though surrounded by the Soviet occupation zone. The Allied response was the celebrated air lift. In the spring of 1949, as part of his apparent shift to a hold-the-line strategy, Stalin abandoned the blockade, but this time Germany was officially and apparently permanently divided between the new Federal Republic (West Germany) and the German Democratic Republic (East Germany). The West Berlin enclave has remained within East Germany as a chronic point of tension: an Allied outpost and escape route for refugees that is in turn vulnerable to Soviet counterpressure.

The Far Eastern power vacuum left by World War II invited a struggle between Communists and anti-Communists that was considerably more prolonged and violent than in the case of Europe. In the Soviet occupation zone of North Korea a Communist Korean People's Democratic Republic was quickly established. In China the prewar Nationalist government, with American support, resumed control of the cities that had been under Japanese occupation and then had to contend with renewed Chinese Communist guerrilla warfare. In 1948 the Nationalists began to crumble, more because of corruption and the failure of morale than from actual military inferiority, and the Communists swept them out of one stronghold after another. In October 1949 the Communists proclaimed the Chinese People's Republic, with Mao Tse-tung as President. Soviet Russia immediately recognized the new regime (even though Stalin, by his own admission, had not expected so quick a takeover), signed a treaty of aid and alliance, and seemed to secure the ideological allegiance of the Chinese.

In 1950 the Soviet Union resorted to a tactic it had rarely used, direct military aggression. Stalin, presumably, gave the go-ahead to his Soviet-equipped North Korean satellite to invade the Republic of Korea to the south. He learned quickly that the United States was prepared to resist any such move by force, when American troops, with UN support, intervened to save South Korea. The Chinese Communists intervened in turn to salvage North Korea, and three years of bitter fighting ensued. Soviet Russia furnished supplies and aircraft to the Chinese—at a price—but remained technically neutral. It was apparently the shift in Russian policy after Stalin died that led the Chinese to conclude a truce in Korea in the summer of 1953. The net result of the war was to transfer the North Korean satellite from the Soviet orbit to the Chinese. This left the leadership of Far Eastern Communism entirely to the Chinese.

By 1949 (1951 in Korea) the partition of the postwar power vacuums in Europe and Asia was complete, and the Soviet bloc expanded no further. Soviet development of an atomic bomb (aided by espionage and by the employment of captured German experts) tightened the stalemate between East and West.

Stalin's death in March 1953 was immediately reflected in a normalization of diplomatic relations and such minor steps as permission for Russian wives of foreigners to leave the country. Soviet military thinkers were allowed for the first time to take real account of the role of atomic weapons and their possibly devastating effect on the Soviet Union as well as on its enemies. Russia produced a hydrogen bomb and the intercontinental rockets to deliver it in the mid-1950s, soon after the United States. Under cover of the nuclear balance of terror, the Russia of Malenkov and Khrushchev undertook a new line of wooing the neutrals and conciliating the enemy. Such was peaceful coexistence, as Khrushchev began to call it.

Peaceful coexistence bore fruit almost immediately in Southeast Asia, where Communist guerrillas in Indochina had been fighting their French colonial rulers since 1946. In 1954 a peace conference in Geneva agreed to partition independent Viet-Nam into a Communist state in the north and a non-Communist state in the south and guaranteed the neutrality of Laos and Cambodia. The truce held up for five or six years, until renewed Communist guerrilla activity in Laos and South Viet-Nam again threw the region into a crisis. In Europe the Soviet Union moved to reduce some of the most acute points of tension by recognizing West Germany (as well as East), agreeing to the evacuation and neutralization of Austria, and mending relations with Tito's Yugoslavia. The new spirit of normal diplomacy was signaled by the 1955 Geneva "summit" conference of heads of state—Bulganin and Khrushchev, Prime Minister Anthony Eden of Great Britain, Premier Edgar Faure of France, and President Eisenhower of the United States.

Within the Communist movement the bold move by Khrushchev to dethrone the memory of Stalin in 1956 touched off a new process of ferment. Where Communist parties were already small, as in the United States and northwest Europe, they began to disintegrate, and elsewhere they were rent by factional battles over the issue of Stalinism. In eastern Europe the prospect of relaxation of Soviet control brought the satellites near the point of open revolt. The crisis materialized first in Poland, with the Poznan workers' riots in the summer of 1956, followed by the decision of the Polish Communists to restore the "national Communist" Gomulka to power as Secretary-General of the Party. Khrushchev flew to Warsaw to protest, but the Poles threatened armed resistance, and actual clashes with Soviet troops occurred. Khrushchev backed down, and Gomulka won the right to pursue an independent internal policy.

More serious was the revolution in Hungary, inspired by the example of Poland's resistance. Late in October 1956 mobs of students clashed with the police in Budapest. The authority of the Communist government broke down in a manner reminiscent of the February Revolution in Russia, complete with spontaneously elected workers' councils. Soviet troops briefly fought the rebels and retired. Much of the Hungarian Communist Party joined the revolution, and the moderate Communist Imre Nagy was made Prime Minister. Nagy proclaimed an end to dictatorship and formed a coalition government with non-Communist leaders. Then he took the fatal step of terminating Hungary's alliance with Soviet Russia and proclaiming his country's neutrality. At this Khrushchev made a quick decision to act. Soviet troops poured back into Hungary, ringed Budapest, and, on November 4, 1956, attacked and overwhelmed the defenders of the Nagy government. Lingering resistance was put down, and Janos Kadar, a Nagy man who had gone over to the Russian side, was installed in power. Kadar was careful, however, to avoid the worst terrors and economic rigors of his predecessors, and by the 1960s Hungary had become the most moderate of the Soviet satellites in eastern Europe.

Possible action in the East European upheaval by Russia's Western antagonists was precluded by a simultaneous crisis in the Near East. When Egypt's President Nasser nationalized the Suez Canal, Israel, Britain, and France retaliated by invading Egypt early in November. Russia and the United States, for once on the same side, opposed the invasion, though Khrushchev went so far as to threaten a rocket attack on London and Paris. Soviet influence rose considerably among the Arab states, until in 1957 the possibility of a

Communist take-over in Syria made a Near Eastern war seem imminent. At this juncture anti-Communist Syrians prevented revolution by accepting the opportunity to federate with Egypt into the United Arab Republic. This caused a break between Egypt and Russia, and the USSR has never fully recovered its influence in the Near East.

The crises in Poland, Hungary, and Suez set Soviet-Western relations back rudely, but from 1957 to 1959 the international atmosphere improved again. Khrushchev reduced his ground army and announced a suspension of atomic weapons testing. The United States and Britain responded by stopping their own tests. In 1959, following an exchange of high-level visits, Khrushchev himself visited the United States, boasted of the ultimate economic victory of Communism, and urged "general and complete disarmament" in the meanwhile. This second East-West *detente* came to grief in 1960 because of Khrushchev's impatience over the Berlin problem, the "U-2 incident" when the Russians downed an American reconnaissance plane deep in Soviet territory, and the collapse of a new summit meeting in Paris.

The period from mid-1960 to the end of 1962 was a time of renewed and acute tension between the Soviet Union and the West. Communist forces began to wage guerrilla warfare again in Southeast Asia and tried to establish political beachheads in some of the newly independent African republics, particularly the strife-torn Congo. The Western presence in Berlin had become more hateful to the Soviets than ever because it allowed so many refugees to flee from East Germany. When tension reached its peak in August 1961, the Communists built the notorious Berlin Wall to cut off all communication between East Germany and West Berlin. Then Russia broke the informal moratorium on nuclear testing and exploded a series of mammoth bombs, presumably to intimidate the West with a display of Soviet power.

The most dangerous situation of the early 1960s was the espousal of Communism by Fidel Castro in Cuba. The growth of Soviet influence in Cuba and of Cuban influence in the rest of Latin America prompted American countermeasures, including the abortive attempt in 1961 to overthrow Castro by landing a force of Cuban refugees at the Bay of Pigs. In mid-1962 Khrushchev ventured to construct a secret Soviet missile base in Cuba within rocket range of the entire United States. When this move was detected, Khrushchev was confronted with an American blockade of Cuba and the threat of American military intervention. He complied by removing the rockets in return for a tacit American agreement not to invade Cuba. The power balance was restored, and the Soviet attitude toward the West abruptly changed to a line of friendly accommodation. The first important fruit of this shift was a formal treaty in August 1963 to ban the further testing of nuclear weapons in the atmosphere.

While Soviet relations with the West were shifting from accord to crisis and back again, the tensions in the Communist bloc set loose by the crisis of 1956 were becoming increasingly serious. The main problem was Communist China. China was never a Soviet satellite but a separate revolutionary power, restricted in its influence only by the magnitude of its economic problems. Mao Tse-tung claimed to be a prophet of Marxism in his own right, though he acknowledged Stalin's higher authority. At first, apart from Korea and Formosa, he leaned more toward a policy of peaceful coexistence than did Stalin. Internally he began with a relatively cautious policy of consolidation and rebuilding. De-Stalinization in 1956 surprised and angered Mao, and in 1957 and 1958 the Chinese struck out on their own with a radical turnabout in both internal and foreign policy. Mao began to challenge Khrushchev's authority in the Communist movement and criticized the Soviet overtures to the West, the neutrals, and the Yugoslav heretics. By 1960 China and Russia were fighting openly in various international Communist meetings. The rift was dramatically underscored when Albania sided with China to win a new protector against Yugoslavia and attacked Khrushchev openly for the sin of "revisionism." Khrushchev broke diplomatic relations with Albania late in 1961 and suspended all Soviet economic and technical aid to China. Undissuaded, the Chinese launched a border war with India in the fall of 1962 despite—or perhaps because of—Khrushchev's friendship with Indian Prime Minister Nehru. Next Mao denounced Khrushchev for softness toward capitalism when he withdrew his missiles from Cuba. By 1963 the Russians and Chinese were openly accusing one another of heretical deviations from Marxism. Their competition for leadership in the international Communist movement produced serious splits in many Communist parties in Western Europe, Latin America, and India. Far Eastern Communists —the governments of North Korea and North Viet-Nam and the Communist parties of Japan and Indonesia—lined up with China. In February 1964 the Chinese compared the Russians to the Social Democrats of 1919 and proclaimed themselves the true heirs of Lenin.

With this trend toward "polycentrism" in the Communist movement the wheel of history had swung full circle. Moscow was no longer the unique center of a revolutionary movement. The Com-

There is a vast amount of reading material by Western scholars on Russia and its history available in English, as well as many Soviet publications in English translation. The present book, of course, is only a bare summary of our knowledge about Russia, and the suggestions for further reading listed here are only representative of the many fine works written for the serious student of Russian affairs.

There are several good, up-to-date American texts covering the entire history of Russia: Jesse Clarkson, A History of Russia (New York: 1961), Nicholas Riazanovsky, A History of Russia (New York: 1963), and Sidney Harcave, Russia: A History (rev. ed., Philadelphia: 1959). B. H. Sumner, A Short History of Russia (rev. ed., New York: 1949), is an interesting topic-by-topic presentation by a British historian. The Soviet view is available in The Outline History of the USSR (Moscow: 1960).

No doubt the best English-language survey of Russian history up to the Revolution is Michael Florinsky, Russia: A History and An Interpretation (2 vols., New York: 1955). Among the classics of Russian historical writing available in English are Vasily Kliuchevsky, A Course of Russian History (5 vols., reprinted, New York: 1960), S. M. Platonov, History of Russia (New York: 1925), and Paul Miliukov, Russia and Its Crisis (reprinted, New York: 1962). Anatol Mazour, Rise and Fall of the Romanovs (Princeton: 1960), is a brief account supplemented by documents, while a broader selection of documents is available in Warren Walsh, ed., Readings in Russian History (3 vols., rev. ed., Syracuse: 1963). Key readings in intellectual history are collected in Hans Kohn, ed., The Mind of Modern Russia (reprinted, New York: 1962).

Detailed studies of every period and problem in Russian history are not always available in English, but the reader may consult George Vernadsky's four volumes of A History of Russia (New Haven: 1943-), which so far cover Russia from ancient times to the sixteenth century. Karl A. Wittfogel's Oriental Despotism (New Haven: 1957) sheds some light on the old Russian government. Tsarist foreign policy is analyzed and compared with Soviet practices in Ivo Lederer, ed., *Russian Foreign Policy* (New Haven: 1962). Peter I. Lyaschchenko, *History of the National Economy of the USSR* (New York: 1949), a Soviet work in translation, is the best available economic history. S. V. Utechin, *Russian Political Thought* (New York: 1963), surveys the intellectual history of the eighteenth and nineteenth centuries. The history of Russian literature up to the present time is well covered in Marc Slonim's two volumes, *The Epic of Russian Literature* (New York: 1950), and *Modern Russian Literature* (New York: 1953).

The decades just before the Revolution are examined in detail by Hugh Seton-Watson in *The Decline of Imperial Russia* (New York: 1952), and by Sir John Maynard in *Russia in Flux* (New York: 1948). The revolutionary movement is surveyed in Avrahm Yarmolinsky, *A Century of Revolution* (reprinted, New York: 1962), and in Franco Venturi, *Roots of Revolution* (New York: 1960). The Bolshevik movement and its setting are treated in Donald Treadgold, *Lenin and His Rivals* (New York: 1955), Leopold Haimson, *The Russian Marxists and the Origins of Bolshevism* (Cambridge, Mass.: 1955), and Bertram Wolfe, *Three Who Made a Revolution* (New York: 1948). Serious work on Lenin has recently begun with two biographies, Louis Fischer, *The Life of Lenin* (New York: 1964), and Stefan Possony, *Lenin: The Compulsive Revolutionary* (Chicago: 1964).

The background of Marxist theory has been exhaustively studied, but the reader might most profitably consult Edmund Wilson, *To The Finland Station* (reprinted, New York: 1953), and G. D. H. Cole, *The Meaning of Marxism* (reprinted, Ann Arbor, Mich.: 1964). The original texts may be studied in the brief selections contained in Sidney Hook, *Marx and the Marxists* (New York: 1955), or in the more extensive anthology by Lewis Feuer, *Marx and Engels: Basic Writings in Politics and Philosophy* (New York: 1959). Marxism's present significance is appraised in Gustav Wetter, *Dialectical Materialism* (New York: 1959), and in Adam Ulam, *The Unfinished Revolution* (New York: 1960). Lenin's development of the theory is presented in his own *Selected Works* (2 vols., Moscow: 1950-1952), and analyzed in Alfred Meyer, *Leninism* (Cambridge, Mass.: 1957).

The standard history of the Russian Revolution is William Henry Chamberlin's *Russian Revolution* (2 vols., New York: 1935). An unofficial but dramatic Communist view is Trotsky's *History of the Russian Revolution* (3 vols., New York: 1932). It may be balanced by N. N. Sukhanov's eye-witness memoir, *The Russian Revolution of 1917* (abridged translation, London: 1955). John S. Curtiss, in *The Russian Revolutions of 1917* (New York: 1957), presents a brief summary with documentary readings. The parallels between the Russian Revolution and the other great revolutions of history are drawn by Crane Brinton in *The Anatomy of Revolution* (rev. ed., New York: 1952).

There are several comprehensive histories of the Soviet period, of which perhaps the most readable and incisive is Frederick Schuman, *Russia Since 1917* (New York: 1957). Leonard Schapiro, in *The Communist Party of the Soviet Union* (New York: 1960), gives a general history concentrating on the central Soviet institution. The same from a contrary viewpoint is supplied in the official Soviet text by Boris Ponomaryov *et al.*, *History of the CPSU* (Moscow: 1960). Another interpretation of Soviet history, centering on the career of Stalin, is Isaac Deutscher, *Stalin: A Political Biography* (New York: 1949). Deutscher is also the author of a monumental biography of Trotsky in three volumes: *The Prophet Armed, The Prophet Unarmed*, and *The Prophet Outcast* (London: 1954-1963).

The first decade of Soviet rule is recounted exhaustively in the six volumes completed to date of E. H. Carr, *A History of Soviet Russia* (New York: 1951-). On the controversies within the Communist Party see Robert V. Daniels, *The Conscience of the Revolution: Communist Opposition in Soviet Russia* (Cambridge, Mass.: 1960). Stalin's chief pronouncements up to 1939 are collected in the various editions of his *Problems of Leninism* (rev. English ed., Moscow: 1953). Trotsky expounds his viewpoint of the Stalin regime in *The Revolution Betrayed* (New York: 1937). Developments since 1934 are presented in John A. Armstrong, *The Politics of Totalitarianism* (New York: 1961).

For economic history see Maurice Dobb, *Soviet Economic Development Since 1917* (New York: 1949), and Alexander Baykov, *The Development of the Soviet Economic System* (Cambridge: 1946). Social history is analyzed in Nicholas Timasheff, *The Great Retreat* (New York: 1946); religion, in John S. Curtiss, *The Russian Church and The Soviet State* (New York: 1953), and in Solomon Schwarz, *The Jews in the Soviet Union* (Syracuse: 1951). The main developments in ideology are sketched by Klaus Mehnert in *Stalin vs. Marx* (London: 1952).

The standard work on the Soviet government is Merle Fainsod, *How Russia Is Ruled* (rev. ed., Cambridge, Mass.: 1963). Soviet law is examined in Harold Berman, *Justice in the USSR* (rev. ed., reprinted, New York: 1963). The police system is treated in Simon Wolin and R. M. Slusser, eds., *The Soviet Secret Police* (New York: 1957). Recent government policies are surveyed in W. W. Kulski, *The Soviet Regime* (rev. ed., Syracuse: 1959), and in Abraham Brumberg, ed., *Russia Under Khrushchev* (New York: 1962). "Kremlinology," the art of interpreting top-level Soviet politics, is well represented by Robert Conquest, *Power and Policy in the USSR* (London: 1961). Current aspects of ideology are analyzed in Robert C. Tucker, *The Soviet Political Mind* (New York: 1963), and in Leonard Schapiro, ed., *The USSR and the Future* (New York: 1963), which includes the text of the 1961 Communist Party program. Policy toward the national minorities is covered in Frederick Barghoorn, *Soviet Russian Nationalism* (New York: 1956). On recent cultural policy see George Gibian, *Interval of Freedom: Soviet Literature During the Thaw* (Minneapolis: 1960).

The Soviet economic system is well described in Alec Nove, *The Soviet Economy* (New York: 1961). For a clear introduction to the statistical appraisal of the Soviet system see Robert W. Campbell, *Soviet Economic Power* (Cambridge, Mass.: 1960). Industrial organization is surveyed in Joseph Berliner, *Factory and Manager in the USSR* (Cambridge, Mass.: 1957). Naum Jasny, *The Socialized Agriculture of the USSR* (Stanford: 1949), is the basic work in that field. Geography and resources are surveyed in Theodore Shabad, *Geography of the USSR* (New York: 1951), and in George Cressey, *How Strong Is Russia: A Geographic Appraisal* (Syracuse: 1954). A good geographical reference is George Goodall, *The Soviet Union in Maps* (Chicago: 1954).

One of the most interesting expositions of everyday Soviet life, based on interviews with refugees, is Raymond Bauer, Alex Inkeles, and Clyde Kluckhohn, *How the Soviet System Works* (Cambridge, Mass.: 1956). Wright Miller's *Russians as People* (New York: 1961) is a penetrating essay. All aspects of the system are examined in Kent Geiger and Alex Inkeles, ed., *Soviet Society: A Book of Readings* (Boston: 1961).

The only comprehensive history of Soviet foreign policy is Robert Warth, *Soviet Russia in World Politics* (New York: 1963). Arthur Adams, ed., *Readings in Soviet Foreign Policy* (Boston: 1961), presents primary and secondary selections on each historical period. No doubt the most original interpretation is George Kennan, *Russia and the West Under Lenin and Stalin* (reprinted, New York: 1961). For a short account with documents see Kennan's *Soviet Foreign Policy, 1917-1941* (Princeton: 1960). The principal periods in the history of Soviet foreign policy are studied in detail in Louis Fischer, *The Soviets in World Affairs* (2 vols., reprinted, Princeton: 1951), for the years to 1929; Max Beloff, *The Foreign Policy of Soviet Russia* (2 vols., London: 1949), covering 1929 to 1941; J. M. Mackintosh, *Strategy and Tactics of Soviet Foreign Policy* (London: 1962), from World War II to 1960; and Marshall Shulman, *Stalin's Foreign Policy Reappraised* (Cambridge, Mass.: 1963). Philip E. Mosely, *The Kremlin and World Politics* (New

York: 1960), is a collection of essays on the Cold War period. Military aspects are covered in Raymond L. Garthoff, *Soviet Strategy in the Nuclear Age* (New York: 1958).

On the Communist movement in general see Robert V. Daniels, *The Nature of Communism* (reprinted, New York: 1963), and *A Documentary History of Communism* (2 vols., reprinted, New York: 1962). A good short history of the movement is Max Salvadori, *The Rise of Modern Communism* (rev. ed., New York: 1963). A more detailed study up to World War II is Franz Borkenau, *World Communism* (reprinted, New York: 1962). Hugh Seton-Watson, *From Lenin to Krushchev: The History of World Communism* (New York: 1960), is comprehensive and up-to-date. Günther Nollau, in *International Communism and World Revolution* (New York: 1961), inquires into the Soviet use of international Communist organizations. On Soviet relations with other Communist countries see Zbigniew Brzezinski, *The Soviet Bloc: Unity and Conflict* (reprinted, New York: 1961). A good short account of Soviet relations with China is Edward Crankshaw, *The New Cold War: Moscow vs. Peking* (Baltimore: 1963), while the backgrounds of the conflict are exhaustively studied in Donald S. Zagoria, *The Sino-Soviet Conflict, 1956-1961* (Princeton: 1962).

Current developments inside Russia and in Russia's foreign relations are well covered in the standard journals on world affairs. Periodicals dealing more specifically with Russia are *The Slavic Review* (Seattle: quarterly), emphasizing history; *The Russian Review* (Hanover, N.H.: quarterly); *The Slavonic and East European Review* (London: semiannual); *Survey* (London: quarterly), concentrating on cultural affairs; *Soviet Studies* (Glasgow: quarterly), a good reference on economic affairs; *Problems of Communism* (Washington: bimonthly). A weekly compendium of translated Soviet articles is available in *The Current Digest of the Soviet Press*. A general reference is Michael Florinsky, ed., *The McGraw-Hill Encyclopedia of Russia and the Soviet Union* (New York: 1961).

The most helpful bibliographies of material on Russia are the following: Charles Morley, *Guide to Research in Russian History* (Syracuse: 1951), David Shapiro, *A Select Bibliography of Works in English on Russian History, 1801-1917* (Oxford: 1962), Philip Grierson, *Books on Soviet Russia, 1917-1942* (London: 1943), R. N. C. Hunt, *Books on Communism* (London: 1959), and Thomas Hammond, *Bibliography of Soviet Foreign Policy and World Communism* (New York: 1964). The *American Bibliography of Slavic and East European Studies* is an annual series published in Bloomington, Ind. Two short but very helpful guides to the literature and its interpretation are available in the pamphlet series issued by the American Historical Association's Service Center for Teachers of History: Alfred Meyer, *Marxism Since the Manifesto* (No. 41, 1961), and George Barr Carson, *Russia Since 1917* (No. 46, 1962).

INDEX

Absolute monarchy, tradition of, 4
Absolutism, 4, 70
Academy of Science, 12, 49
Acculturation, 50-53
Air lift, 135
Albania, 6, 134, 139
Alexander I, Tsar, 31, 38
Alexander II, Tsar, 39-40, 43, 61
Alexander III, Tsar, 40, 61, 62
Alexandra, Empress, 70, 72
"All Power to the Soviets," 75
Altai mountains, 3
Amur river, 33
Andreev, Andrei, 116
Anglo-American aid, 118, 131
Anna, Empress, 38
April Theses, 75
Arctic ocean, 3
Armenia, 14, 91
Army of Liberation, 116
Army, Russian, 77-78
Art of the proletariat, 113
Atomic bomb, 136
Austria, 32, 71, 132, 136
Autocracy, 33-40, 54, 97
Axis powers, 5
Azerbaijan, 14-15, 91

Bakunin, Mikhail, 52, 60-61, 66
Baku oil fields, 62
Baltic sea, 3, 30
Baptists, 25
Battle of Tannenberg, 71
Bay of Pigs, 138
Beria, Lavrenty, 110, 119
Bering sea, 3
Berlin wall, 138
Bernstein, Eduard, 66
Bessarabia (Moldavian Republic), 15, 31, 92, 130
Bicameral legislature (Supreme Soviet), 13, 110

Black sea, 3, 27, 28, 30, 31, 44, 91
Bloody Sunday massacre, 69
Blum, Leon, 129
Bogolubsky, Prince Andrei, 29
Bolshevism, 8, 9, 48, 58-95, 112
Boyar Duma (council), 36, 69-70, 72
Brest-Litovsk, treaty of, 86, 87, 88, 91
Brezhnev, Leonid, 12, 121, 124
British Labour Party, 65
Bukharin, Nikolai, 86, 99, 100, 102, 104, 109
Bulganin, Nikolai, 116, 119, 120-121, 136
Bulgaria, 6, 132, 134
Byelorussia, 3, 14, 25, 28, 30, 91, 92

Cambodia, 136
Caspian sea, 3
Castro, Fidel, 138
Catherine II, the Great, 31, 38, 42, 44, 60
Catholic Church of the Eastern Rite, see Uniate Church
Catholics, Roman, 25, 28, 48, 49
Central Committee, 12, 98-99
Central Executive Committee of the Soviets (CEC), 82
Centralized economic control, 105
Cheka, see Extraordinary Commission to Combat Counterrevolutionary Activities
Chekhov, Anton, 51
Chernyshevsky, Nikolai, 52, 61
Chiang Kai-shek, 126
Chicherin, Georgi, 126
China, 6, 26, 68. See also Chinese People's Republic.
Chinese People's Republic, 126-127, 135, 139
Christian Church, 25
Chubar, Vlas, 109
Church Slavonic, 28, 46

Churchill, Winston, 132
Civil War, 88-89, 92
Collective farms (*kolkhozy*), 17, 19, 106-107, 118
"Collective leadership," 119
Cominform, *see* Communist Information Bureau
Comintern, *see* Communist International
Commission of Party and State Control, 12
Committee of State Security (KGB), 16, 84
Communism, outside Russia, 5-6
Communist Central Committee, 88
Communist China, *see* Chinese People's Republic
Communist Information Bureau (Cominform), 134
Communist International (Comintern), 5, 128-129, 132
Communist League of 1848-1852, 65
Communist Manifesto (Karl Marx), 64
Communist Party of Russia, apparatus of, 10, 11, 12; bureaucratic organization of, 98; centralization of authority, 18; membership in, 10; monopoly of education, 9; monopoly of government offices, 106; monopoly of mass media, 9; power structure of, 10-11; pre-eminence of under Khrushchev, 120; sources of, 9; system of circular control, 11; "troika" leadership of, 99
Communist Party Program, 122
Congo, 138
Congress Kingdom of Poland, 32
Congress of Berlin, 32
Congress of the Communist International, 89
Congress of Vienna, 31-32
Constantinople, 28, 29
Constitutional Democratic Party (Kadets), 62-63, 70, 76, 80
Constitutions, 12-13, 82, 110
"Corrective labor camps," 107
Cossacks, 30, 37, 69, 76, 84
Council of People's Commissars, 13-14, 82, 83, 99, 100, 110
Council of State, 69
Crimean war, 31, 32, 39

Cromwell, Oliver, 58
Cuba, 138-139
"Cult of personality," 120
Culture, 21-23, 45-53, 111-112
Curzon Line, 92, 133
Cyrillic alphabet, 46, 50
Czechoslovak Legion, 87
Czechoslovakia, 6, 128, 129, 132, 134

Das Kapital, 66
"Decembrists," 38-39, 60
Democratic humanism, 9
Denikin, General, 91
Dictatorship of the proletariat, 122-123
Dimitrov, Georgi, 128
Divorce, 114
Doctor Zhivago (Boris Pasternak), 23
"Doctors' Plot," 119
Donets Basin, 62, 118
Donskoi, Prince Dmitri, 29
Dostoevsky, Fedor, 39, 51, 53

East Germany, 6, 134
Eden, Anthony, 136
Education, 24-26, 114, 122
Egypt, 137-138
Eisenhower, Dwight D., 136
Elizabeth, Empress, 38
Emancipation of serfs, 43, 77
Engels, Friedrich, 22, 64, 65, 66
England, *see* Great Britain
Equality of sexes, 21
Estonia, 15, 31, 50, 91, 92, 130
Evergreen forests (*taiga*), 3
Extraordinary Commission to Combat Counterrevolutionary Activities (Cheka), 84

Famine, 107-108, 118
Fascism, 9, 127
Federal Republic of Germany (West Germany), 135. *See also* Germany.
Finland, 31, 44, 86, 130
First Comintern Congress, 90
First Five-Year Plan, 18, 105, 106, 108, 112
Formosa, 139
Fourth International of Trotskyist parties, 103
France, 5, 6, 31-32, 33, 69, 71, 88, 91, 128-131, 137
Franco, Francisco, 129

Franz Ferdinand, Archduke, 71
Free love, 21, 112
French Revolution, 48, 51, 56, 57, 60, 88
Frontiers, natural, 3

Georgia, 14, 25, 91
German Democratic Republic (East Germany), 135. *See also* Germany.
Germany, 5, 6, 33, 56, 57, 65, 69, 71, 75, 78, 85-86, 87, 89, 127-132, 135
Gogol, Nikolai, 51
Gorky, Maxim, 109
Gosplan (State Planning Commission), 104-105
Great Britain, 5, 33, 65, 69, 71, 88, 91, 126, 128, 129, 137
Great Northern War, 30-31
Great Russians, 14, 25, 28
Greece, 131, 134
Guchkov, Alexander, 73
Gudonov, Boris, 36

Herzen, Alexander, 52, 60
Hitler, Adolph, 58, 117, 127, 129, 131
Holy Alliance, 31
Hungary, 6, 132, 134, 137

India, 2, 139
Indochina, 136
Industrial Revolution, 42-43, 55, 59
Industry, state-owned, 17-18
Intelligentsia, the, 51-52, 60
International Communism: discrepancy between theory and practice, 9; effect on expansion of Russian power, 5; revolutionary movement of, 5-6; varieties of, 9
International Workingmen's Association (First International), 65
Israel, 137
Italy, 5
Ivan III, 29-30, 35
Ivan IV, 30, 36

Jacobins, 58
Japan, 5, 33, 68, 69, 88, 132
Jews, 16, 25, 47, 48, 49, 89, 117, 122

Kadar, Janos, 137
Kadets, *see* Constitutional Democratic Party

Kaganovich, Lazar, 116, 119, 121
Kalinin, Mikhail, 99, 102, 116
Kamenev, Leo, 75, 79, 86, 99, 102, 108
Kandinsky, Vasili, 53
Kautsky, Karl, 66
Kazakhstan, 15
Kerensky, Alexander, 74, 76, 78, 80, 81
KGB (Committee of State Security), 84
Khan, Batu, 29
Khan, Genghis, 29
Khrushchev, Nikita, 10, 11, 12, 14, 22, 25, 96, 109, 116, 119-124, 136
Kiev, 28-30, 34, 46, 48
Kievan society, 40
Kirgizia, 15
Kirilenko, Andrei, 12, 124
Kirov, Sergei, 108
Kolchak, Admiral, 91
Kolkhozy, see collective farms
Kollontai, Alexandra, 93
Korea, 33, 132, 135, 139
Kornilov, General Lavr, 76
Kosior, Stanislav, 109
Kosygin, Alexei, 12
Kozlov, Frol, 12, 121
Kuibyshev, Valerian, 109
Kulaks, 70, 97, 107
Kulikovo, Battle of, 29
Kurile Islands, 33
Kuusinen, Otto, 121

Labor, conditions of, 105-106
Laos, 136
Latvia, 15, 31, 50, 92, 130
League of Nations, 128
Lenin, Vladimir (Nikolai), 9, 12, 22, 67, 68, 72, 75, 76-78, 79-100
Leningrad Affair, 115
Leninism, 7. *See also* Marxism-Leninism.
Literacy, 23
Lithuania, 15, 30, 71-72, 92, 130
Litvinov, Maxim, 116, 128, 129
Lomonosov, Mikhail, 50
Lutherans, 25, 49
Lvov, Prince Georgi, 73, 74

Malenkov, Georgi, 115-116, 117, 118, 119, 121, 136

Malinovsky, Marshal Rodion, 121
Manchuria, 33, 69, 132
Manuilsky, Dmitri, 104
Mao Tse-tung, 127, 135, 139
Marx, Karl, 22, 52, 64, 66, 96
Marxism, 63-68
Marxism-Leninism, 22-26, 55, 59, 63-68, 87, 95, 97, 102, 115
Mendeleyev's Periodic Law, 51
Mendelian theory, 23
Mensheviks, 67, 74, 75, 77, 80, 83
Metropolitan (of the Church), 29, 46
Mexican Revolution, 56
MGB (Ministry of State Security), 84
Mikoyan, Anastas, 12, 13, 116, 119, 121
Military Revolutionary Committee, 79-80
Miliukov, Paul, 70, 73, 74
Ministry of Internal Affairs (MVD), 16, 84
Ministry of State Security (MGB), 84
Modernism, 53
Moldavian Republic, see Bessarabia
Molotov, Vyacheslav, 94, 99, 102, 104, 110, 116, 119, 121, 129-130
Mongols, 3-4, 28, 29, 33, 35, 40, 46. See also Tartars.
Moscow, 29, 47, 62, 69, 84, 86, 91, 104, 139
Moscow Trials, 108-109
Moslems, 25, 49
Munich agreement, 129
MVD, see Ministry of Internal Affairs

Nagy, Imre, 137
Napoleonic wars, 31, 48, 51
Nasser, Gamal, 137
Nechaev, Sergei, 61
NEP, see New Economic Policy
Nepmen, 98, 101, 106
Neutral nations, 7
New Deal, the, 128
New Economic Policy (NEP), 93, 96, 97, 98, 112, 118
Newspapers, 9
Nicholas I, Tsar, 38-39
Nicholas II, Tsar, 40, 54, 61, 69, 72, 89
Nihilism, 61
Nikon, Patriarch, 48

NKVD, see People's Commissariat of Internal Affairs
Norsemen (Varangians), 28
North Korea, 6, 132, 139
North Viet-Nam, 139
Novgorod, 28, 34, 35
Nuclear stockpiles, 7

October manifesto, 69
October Revolution, 77, 82, 85
Okhotsk, sea of, 3
Old Believers, 25, 48
Ordzhonikidze, Sergei, 109
Organizational Bureau (Orgburo), 89, 118
Orgburo, see Organizational Bureau
Outer Mongolia, 6, 91-92

Pacific ocean, 3, 30
Pasternak, Boris, 23, 122
Patriarch of Moscow, 25, 48
Peaceful coexistence, 136, 139
Peasant movements, 77, 107
People's Commissariat of Internal Affairs (NKVD), 84, 110
People's Courts, 16
"Peoples' democracies," 134
Pervukhin, Mikhail, 119
Pestel, Colonel Paul, 60
Peter I, the Great, 30-31, 37, 42, 48, 54, 60, 62
Petrograd, 72, 73, 76, 77, 78, 81, 83, 91
Piatakov, Grigory, 108
Plekhanov, Georgi, 66
Podgorny, Nikolai, 12, 124
Pogroms, 89
Pokrovsky, Mikhail, 114
Poland, 6, 31, 36, 44, 71-72, 86, 92, 130, 132, 133-134, 136
Police, secret, 16, 54, 70, 84, 119
Politburo (Political Bureau), 88-89, 99, 108, 116. See also Presidium of the Supreme Soviet.
Political Bureau, see Politburo
Polkovnikov, Colonel, 80
Polyansky, Dmitri, 12
Poniatowski, Stanislas, 31
Popular Front, 128-129, 132, 133
Population statistics, 44-45
Populism, 52-53, 61, 63, 66, 67, 77
Potsdam Conference, 132, 134-135

Poznan workers' riots, 137
Preobrazhensky, E. A., 102
Presidium of the Supreme Soviet, 12, 13, 110, 118. See also Politburo.
Primary Party Organization (P.P.O.), 10
Procurator General, 16
Proletarian culture, 112
Proletarian revolution, 22, 63, 65, 66, 67, 75, 86, 87, 96
Prussia, 32
Pskov, 35
Pugachov (rebel leader), 42
Purge, the Great, 108-109
Puritan Revolution, 56, 57
Pushkin, Aleksander, 39, 51

Quadruple Alliance, 31

Radek, Karl, 108
Radishchev, Alexander, 60
Rasputin, Grigory, 70, 72
Red army, 87, 90, 91, 92
Red Terror, 89
Religion, 24-25
Republic of Korea (South Korea), 135-136
Revolution, Russian, 4, 56-95, 112, 125-126
Right Opposition, 103-104
Romanov, Mikhail, 36
Roosevelt, Franklin D., 132
Rumania, 6, 92, 132, 134
Russia, see Union of Soviet Socialist Republics
Russian Communist Party, see Communist Party of Russia
Russian national state, 3-4
Russian Orthodox Church, 24-25, 28, 46, 83, 114-115, 122
Russian Social Democratic Workers' Party, 63
Russian Socialist Federated Soviet Republic, 14
Russo-Japanese War, 33
Rykov, Alexei, 99, 100, 104, 109

Saburov, Maxim, 119, 121
St. Petersburg, 31, 62, 69
Sarai (city), 35
Schumpeter, Joseph, "The Sociology of Imperialism," 71

Sea of Japan, 3
Second Congress of the Soviets, 79, 81, 82
Second Five-Year Plan, 105, 108
Second International, 65-66
Serfdom, 41
Seven-Year Plan, 18, 121-122
Shvernik, Nikolai, 12, 104
Siberia, 2, 3, 30, 91, 107
Sino-Soviet dispute, 6
Smolny (district), 81
Social Democratic Party, 66-67, 68, 69, 70
Social thought, 112-113
Socialist realism, 117
Socialist Revolutionary Party (SR's), 63, 69, 74, 77, 80, 83, 88
Sokolnikov, Grigory, 108
Solzhenitsyn, Alexander, 122
Sorel, Georges, 66
South Sakhalin, 33
Southern Society, 60
Soviet of Nationalities (upper house), 13
Soviet of the Union (lower house), 13
Soviet Union, see Union of Soviet Socialist Republics
Sovkhoz (state farm), 20
Spain, 6, 129
Spanish Civil War, 129
Speransky, Mikhail, 38
Sputnik, 121
Stakhanovite movement, 105-106
Stalin, Joseph, 7, 11, 12, 16, 18, 19, 22, 23, 53, 58, 75, 79, 82, 84, 92, 94-120, 127-133, 136
Stalin Revolution, 96, 104-115
Stalingrad, battle of, 131-132
Stalinism, case against, 120-121
State and Revolution (N. Lenin), 76
State capitalism, 93
State farm (sovkhoz), 20
State Labor Reserves, 118
State Planning Commission (Gosplan), 104-105
State Political Administration (GPU), 84
State socialism, 17-25
Stolypin, Peter, 70
Stravinsky, Igor, 53
Suslov, Mikhail, 12, 121

Sviatoslav, Prince, 28
Sweden, 30, 36

Taiga, (evergreen forests), 3
Tajikistan, 15
Tartars, 16, 41. *See also* Mongols.
Taxes, 20
Tenth Communist Party Congress, 93
Tereshchenko, Mikhail, 74
Testament of Lenin, 99
Theory of relativity, 23
Thermidorean Reaction of the Russian Revolution, 93
Third Five-Year Plan, 118
"Third revolution," 93
Tito, Marshal, 6, 120, 134
Tolstoy, Leo, 39, 51
Tomsky, Michael, 98, 99, 104, 109
Totalitarianism, 8, 54, 59
Trade Unions, 18, 88, 98
Transcaucasia, 3, 27, 31
Treaty of Riga, 92
Triple Entente, 71
Trotsky, Leon, 69, 75, 79, 82, 83, 86-88, 89-90, 99, 100-103, 127: "Theory of Permanent Revolution," 85
Trotskyists, 94, 102, 127
Tsarism, origins of, 4, 7, 36
Tukhachevsky, Mikhail, 109
Turgenev, Ivan, 51
Turkey, 30, 32, 86
Turkmenia, 15

Ukraine, the, 3, 14, 25, 28, 30, 84, 86, 91, 92
Uncommitted nations, 7-8
Uniate Church (Catholic Church of the Eastern Rite), 47
Union of Soviet Socialist Republics: agriculture of, 97; armed might of, 6-7; as a landlocked power, 3; business in, 3; central government organization of, 3-4; climate of, 2-3; creation of, 14, 91; economic and cultural lag, 4-5; elections in, 14; historical roots of, 1; intellectual life of, 3; multinational character of, 14, 27-45; nationalization of industry, 90; population of, 2; private property in, 3; public puritanism of, 114; relationship of to world-wide Communism, 1, 125; religion in, 3; satellite governments of, 6; states of, 91; territorial resources of, 2; unification of, 91; universities of, 24
United Arab Republic, 138
United Nations, 132
United States of America, 2, 5, 19, 33, 88, 120
University of Moscow, 50
Ural mountains, 3, 62
Utopia, 22-23, 57, 60, 65, 90, 93, 122
"U-2 incident," 138
Uzbekistan, 15

Varangians (Norsemen), 28
Viet-Nam, 136
Viking Riurik, 28
Vladimir, Prince, 28
Vladivostok, 33
Vlasov, General Andrei, 116
Voronov, Gennady, 12
Voroshilov, Klementy, 102, 116, 119

Wages, 90, 98
War Communism, 90, 92, 97, 98, 112
War Industry Committees, 72
Weimar Republic, 127
West Berlin, 135
West Germany, 120, 135, 136
White Russia, *see* Byelorussia
White sea, 3
Whites, the, 87, 88, 89, 91, 114
Witte, Count Sergei, 69
Workers' and Peasants' Red Army, 88
World War I, 70-72, 85
World War II, 5, 6, 7, 18, 45, 92, 115, 128-133
Wrangel, Baron, 91

Yagoda, Henrykh, 109
Yalta agreement, 132, 134-135
Yaroslav the Wise, Prince, 28-29
Yevtushenko, Yevgeny, 23, 122
Yezhov, Nikolai, 109-110
Yudenich, General, 91
Yugoslavia, 6, 120, 131, 132, 133, 134, 136, 139

Zemsky Sobor, 36
Zhdanov, Andrei, 115, 117, 134
Zhukkov, Marshal Georgi, 120, 121, 132
Zinoviev, Grigory, 79, 86, 99, 100, 102, 108